MW01025638

PALETTE
mini

TRANSPARENT

20th Anniviction:ary

First published and distributed by
viction:workshop ltd.

viction:ary™

viction:workshop ltd.
Unit C, 7/F, Seabright Plaza, 9-23 Shell Street,
North Point, Hong Kong
Url: victionary.com
Email: we@victionary.com
 @victionworkshop
 @victionworkshop
Bē @victionary
 @victionary

Edited and produced by viction:ary

Creative direction by Victor Cheung
Book design by viction:workshop ltd.
Typeset in NB International Pro from Neubau

©2021 viction:workshop ltd.
All rights reserved. No part of this publication may be
reproduced, stored in retrieval systems, or transmitted
in any form or by any electronic or mechanical means,
including but not limited to photocopying, recording, or any
information storage methods, without written permission
from the respective copyright owners.

All copyrights on text and design work are held by the
respective designers and contributors. All artwork and
textual information in this book are based on the materials
offered by the designers whose work have been included.
While every effort has been made to ensure their accuracy,
viction:workshop ltd. does not accept any responsibility,
under any circumstances, for any errors or omissions.

ISBN 978-988-74628-9-7
Printed and bound in China

PREFACE

According to the Cambridge Dictionary, the word 'palette' may refer to the range of colours that an artist usually paints with on a canvas. Today, however, more than just the primary means of creative expression for wielders of the physical brush, its role has expanded to include that of an important digital tool for crafting meaningful solutions in design. On top of manifesting pure works of the imagination as it has always done, the palette has become a purveyor of infinite visual possibilities with the power to bridge art and commerce. Since the release of its first edition in 2012, viction:ary's PALETTE colour-themed series has become one of the most successful and sought-after graphic design reference collections for students and working professionals around the world; showcasing a thoughtful curation of compelling ideas and concepts revolving around the palette featured. In keeping with the needs and wants of the savvy modern reader, the all-new PALETTE mini Series has been reconfigured and rejuvenated with fresh content, for all intents and purposes, to serve as the intriguing, instrumental, and timeless source of inspiration that its predecessor was, in a more convenient size.

INTRO

According to Wikipedia, transparency allows light to pass through a material without an 'appreciable scattering' of the light, which differs slightly from translucency where the light is refracted to the point of iridescence. Both concepts result in distinct visual styles that are universally appealing, seeing as human-beings have been drawn to light since the dawn of humankind and result in beautiful works of art when manipulated in creative ways. In terms of design, transparency has been one of the most effective ways for designers to create a focal point, a sense of lightness or depth in their work due to its physical properties. By playing with opacity levels, which are directly related to how transparent an object is, they can experiment by blending colours and images through software to push their visuals to the next level. Communication-wise, it has been said that absence can be just as powerful as presence. Through transparency, viewers can be guided to the right message at the right time – depending on the elements that are revealed or concealed.

All the projects in this book highlight various means with which transparency can be utilised to add multiple dimensions to visuals in art or graphic design. In contrast, it can also be a clever means to invoke the spirit of limitlessness. Yana

Makarevich's award-winning identity design for AnotherArt.com (PP. 196-205) features transparent stationery like name cards and documents, alluding to the blank canvas and open possibilities in art. When stacked together upright, the name cards also form a 3D work of art in itself when viewed from different angles. Similarly, Youhyeon Cho's BLANK OBJECT (PP. 568-579) was inspired by experiments with glass and its materiality. The project was enriched by the collection of personal stories on people who constantly make and unmake their boundaries, echoing the 'boundless' properties of glass itself. For the Buddhist Sutra Reconstruction of Water (PP. 018-023), Taiwanese designer Shun-Zhi Yang was influenced by the olden rituals of early Buddhists who had to engrave the teachings of the Buddhist scriptures on slates to inherit the spirit of the sect, passed down through devout rituals over time. Type design and the Buddha Bead, an important Buddhism device, were used as the starting points for conceptualisation – further enhanced with water droplets to symbolise purity.

Transparency can emanate a beautiful sense of fragility reminiscent of the fleetingness of life itself. As part of her Afterlife series, artist Luna Ikuta stripped away the colours and chlorophyll from California poppies by developing a method of isolating the extracellular matrix of a tissue from its inhabiting cells to immortalise them as a ghostly aquatic garden (PP. 408-417). By allowing viewers to see the remaining cell structures that make up the wildflower, she highlighted the delicate nature of plants in a striking way. Floating Vase / RIPPLE, the first commercial product by award-winning design studio oodesign / Taku Omura (PP. 024-027), is shaped like a ripple and floats around on water with the help of air movement. Coupled with the fact that each vase is fit for one flower only, the transparent material gives it the illusion of elegant fluidity. For stpmj's Invisible Barn (PP. 598-603), reflective film formed a major part of its design proposal to recontextualise the landscape of the project site. Placed in the middle of the grove, its barn-shaped wooden structure was sheeted to reflect its surrounding environment like the sky, trees, ground as well as the changing seasons – making the building appear invisible.

In addition to being a medium with which to explore materiality within the physical world, transparency is fast becoming a crucial element in digital design, especially in UI/UX where it can denote different interactive states for users. No matter what happens in the future trends-wise, it will always be a flexible creative facet that packs a punch.

上善若水

謝明諺
Minyen Hsieh

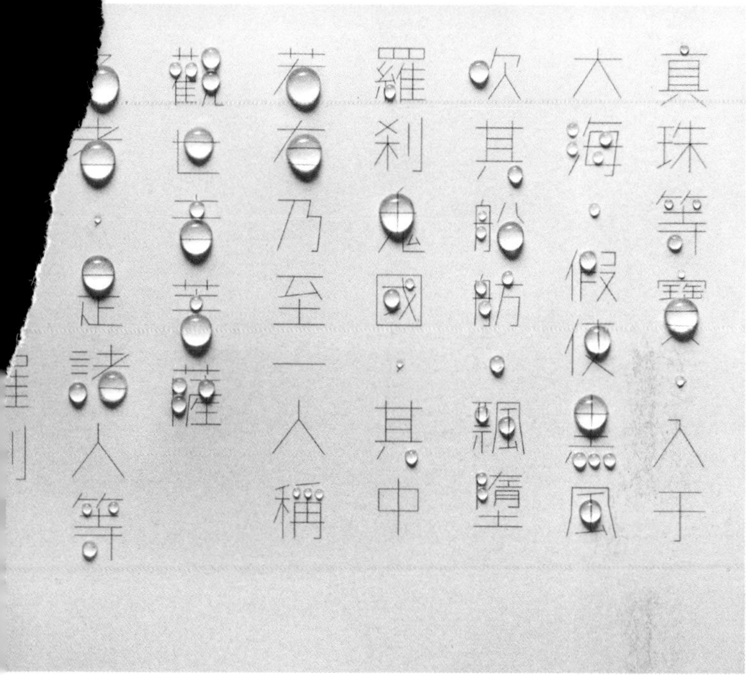

真珠等寶，入于
大海，假使黑風
吹其船舫，飄墮
羅剎鬼國，其中
若有乃至一人稱
觀世音菩薩
名者，是諸人等
羅剎

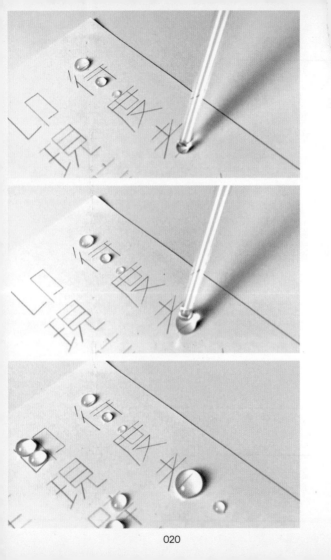

Entre 20 Aguas
A la música
de Paco
de Lucía

*"Paco de Lucía
ha ennoblecido
el flamenco, ha
ampliado su registro,
ha abierto ventanas
por donde otros
deben respirar."*

de interpretación, y un guitarrista tan creativo como Paco con frecuencia ampliaba sus propias versiones de los palos flamencos, aportando material de partitura musical.

Que venía, faltó, aún Paco está sin partitura tomado otros derroteros, aún Paco está sin partitura tomado Manolo de Huelva, como quizás otro cabello había tomado Manolo del mismo Ramón de Algeciras, con una Amado del mismo Ramón—supongo que fue un gran estímulo para el mismo Ramón—supongo que fue un gran estímulo para el mismo Ramón—supongo que fue un en la relación y admiración mutua. Lo hizo, en mi opinión, con una estudie te relación y admiración mutua. Lo hizo, en mi opinión, con una donde le relación de pareja. Entroncan los enseña y se estudie te relación y admiración mutua. Entroncan los enseña y se donde le relación de pareja. En otra manera.

En aquellos años vive más y más tarde en las películas que se sobre aquellos años vive más y más tarde en las creación en sobre aquellos. Carmen, y otros juntos, Paco fue y más escuchado. Perdimos el patrimonio, se le veía más la sensación de que, a través del público que se sienten acomodar fuera del mundo, a eso, aquellos que sobreasalían se sienten solo a fuera del mundo, aquellos que sobreasalían se sienten descolocar en un mundo, aquellos que sobreasalían se sienten siempre ha habido y más grande hasta la atenuación, y lo mismo a Antonio Gades. Y hasta la atenuación, y lo mismo a Antonio Gades. Hoyos, Sara Baras y a tantos otros cantaores, guitarristas y bailaores del mundo.

Paco sea respetado en todo el mundo, el flamenco, ha ampliado su registro, ha abierto ventanas por donde otros deben respirar, y tando de que el flamenco sea algo vivo y no la mortaja que algunos ortodoxos le quieren imponer.

entre
Aguas
a música
Paco
Lucía

EL PAÍS

UNIVERSAL
MUSIC GROUP

casa
limón

PRISA RADIO

© Pepe Lamarca / elbaúm

Entre 20 Aguas

A la música de Paco de Lucía

Abraham Laboriel, Alain Pérez,
Alejandro Sanz, Antonio Sánchez,
Antonio Serrano, Carles Benavent,
Chick Corea, Chucho Valdés,
Dhafer Youssef, Diego del Morao, Ivan Lins,
Jerry González, Jorge Pardo, José Mercé,
Josemi Carmona, Luis Salinas,
Michel Camilo, Pepe de Lucía,
Raimundo Amador, Tino di Geraldo.
Una producción dirigida
por Javier Limón.

Sobre Paco de Lucía
Carlos Saura

Los grandes intérpretes se hacen en edades tempranas y solo con los años adquieren el peso necesario. Paco aprendió a tocar la guitarra de niño en una familia en donde se cultivaba el instrumento y rodeado de amantes del flamenco. No es de extrañar que con tantos grandes músicos, compositores e intérpretes comenzara su andadura a través de las enseñanzas familiares y en un caldo de cultivo privilegiado para el marcador que iba a ser su profesión de por vida. Así, compositores e intérpretes suelen comenzar el aprendizaje a temprana edad. Se dice que la música, como las matemáticas o la física, son conocimientos que se adquieren cuando el cerebro todavía conserva una permeabilidad que más tarde perderemos.

Conocí a Paco de Lucía a través de Antonio Gades para que interviniera en nuestra película Carmen. Lo que más me impresionó de él fue que retomó de la ópera un fragmento conocido y enseguida lo ensambló y lo hizo suyo con esa facilidad que tenía para la improvisación, algo que luego desarrolló siempre con talento.

Para hacer, interpretar música, tocar la guitarra como lo hacía Paco, no basta con valer para ello sino que son necesarias horas y horas de trabajo y una buena dosis de capacidad de sacrificio. Lo sé de buena tinta porque mi madre, que fue pianista profesional, decía que sí un día dejaba de tocar, lo notaba en la digitalización al día siguiente.

La música, que tanta satisfacción procura a quien la interpreta y a los oyentes que la escuchan, es esclava de la perfección, y la única manera de conseguirlo es con el continuo ejercicio. Es cierto que el mundo del flamenco difiere de la música clásica y permite una mayor libertad

"Paco de Lucía ha ennoblecido el flamenco, ha ampliado su registro, ha abierto ventanas por donde otros deben respirar."

de interpretación, y un guitarrista tan creativo como Paco con frecuencia desarrollaba sus propias versiones de los palos flamencos, añadiendo material de su cosecha.

Que se sepa Paco no leía una partitura musical, no le hacía falta, aunque quizá con ello hubiera borrado ciertos derroteros, como su compañero y famoso guitarrista Manolo Sanlúcar, aun así interpretó el Concierto de Aranjuez, del maestro Rodrigo —supongo que fue un desafío consigo mismo—. La hizo, en mi opinión, con una gran sabiduría y personalidad. Entonces los puristas vieron en la interpretación de Paco una intromisión en caminos en donde la música se hace de otra manera: se aprende y se estudia en los conservatorios.

En aquellos años de Carmen y más tarde en las películas que sobre flamenco hicimos juntos, Paco fue creciendo como artista y como persona, se la veía más y más centrado, más recogido, más aislado: siempre tuve la sensación de que, a pesar del bullicioso mundo que suele acompañar al flamenco, aquellos que sobresalen se aíslan y solo a fuerza de tesón, trabajo y sabiduría consiguen descollar en un mundo competitivo en donde por suerte siempre ha habido y hay grandes virtuosos.

He visto a Antonio Gades ensayar hasta la extenuación, y lo mismo a Cristina Hoyos, a Sara Baras y a tantos otros cantaores, guitarristas y bailaores que han hecho que hoy el flamenco sea respetado en todo el mundo.

Paco de Lucía ha ennoblecido el flamenco, ha ampliado su registro, ha abierto ventanas por donde otros deben respirar, tratando de que el flamenco sea algo vivo y no la mortaja que algunos cofrades le quieren imponer.

© Pepe Lamarca / Album

Entre 20 Aguas
A la música de Paco de Lucía

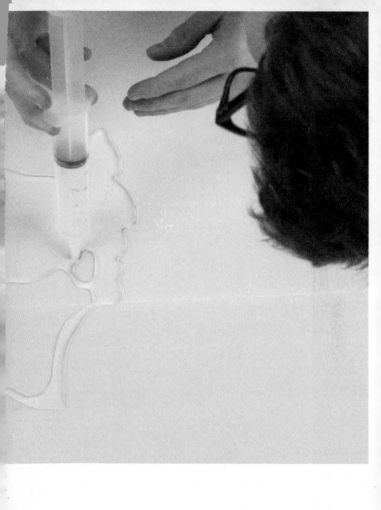

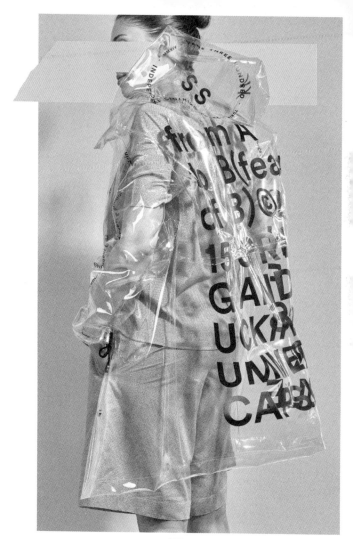

PRESENTADO POR FONDEADORA

BLOP FESTIVAL
DE DISEÑO
& CULTURA

DIC 202✳
CDMX—BCN—BS
13 EXPOSITORXS
BLOP.MX

MARTA CERDA
HEY STUDIO
SIXNFIVE
GOLDTRON
MARIANO PASCUAL
RENÉ & NORMAN
SCARLETT LINDEMAN
IOL
ASHBY SOLANO
NOSOTROS CINCO
VERO ESCALANTE
EMME CARRANZA
ANESA KRONOOL

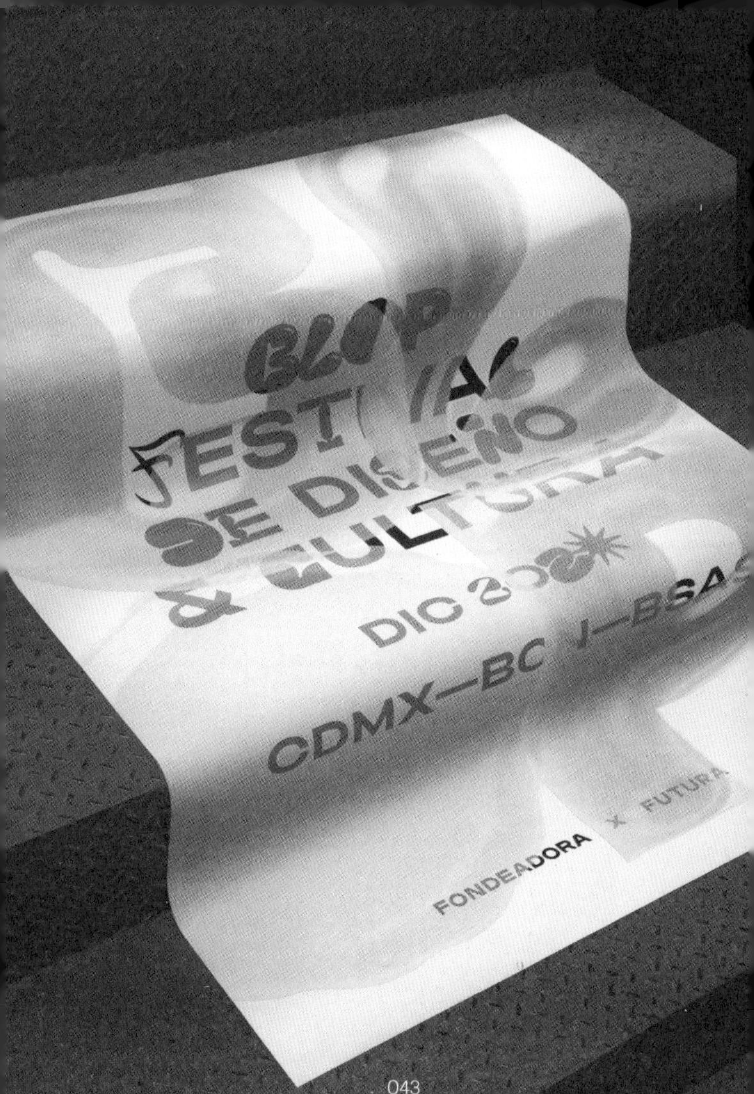
DIC
CDMX—BC
FONDEADORA
X
FUTURA

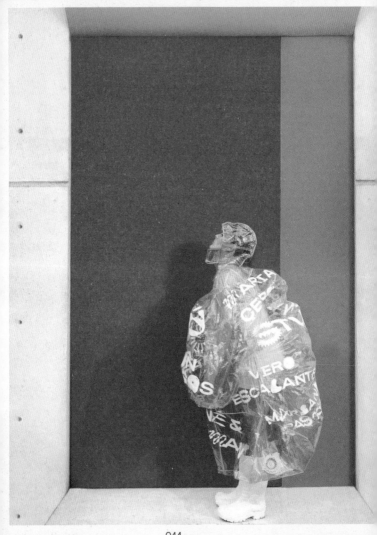

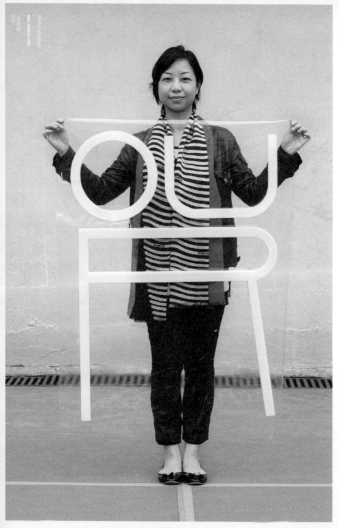

**THE FASHION WORLD
OF JEAN PAUL GAULTIER:
From the Sidewalk
to the Catwalk
15/6-22/9**

Arkitekturmuseet

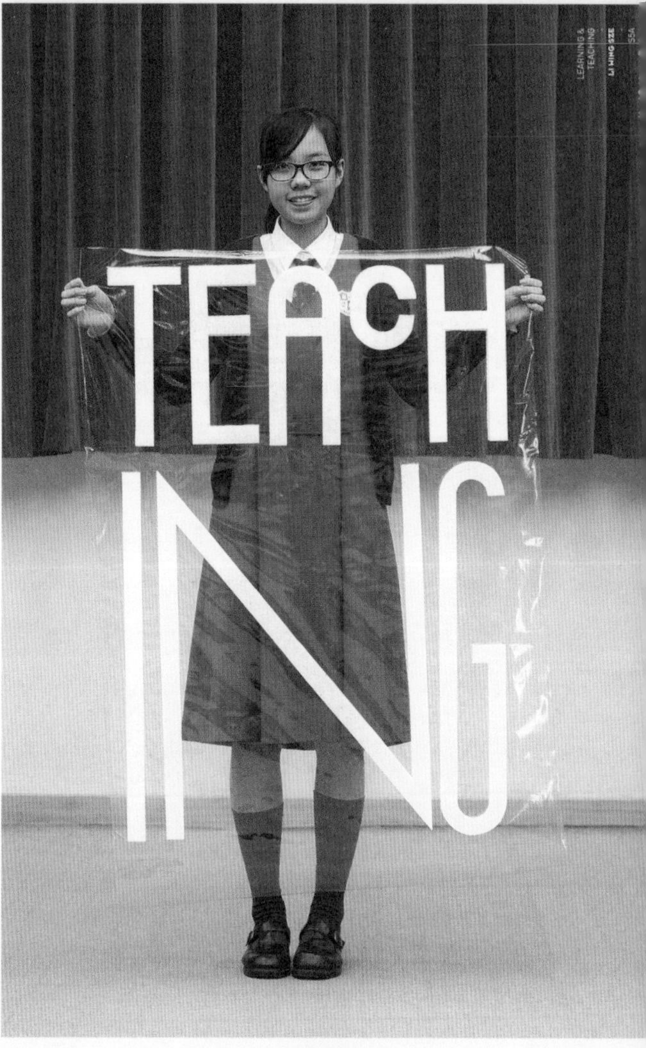
TEACH
ING

THE FASHION WORLD
OF JEAN PAUL GAULTIER:
From the Sidewalk
to the Catwalk
15/6-22/9

Arkitekturmuseet

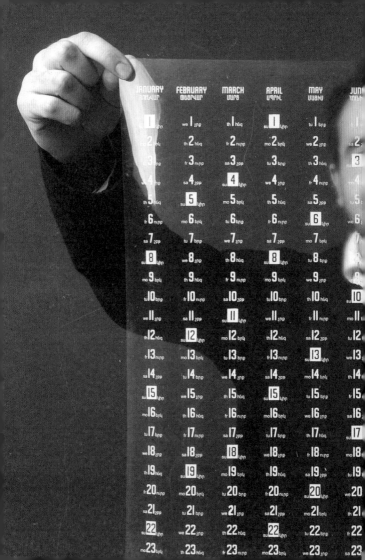

JULY ԼՆ	AUGUST ՕԳՈՍՏՈՍ	SEPTEMBER ՍԵՊՏԵՄԲԵՐ	OCTOBER ՀՈԿՏԵՄԲԵՐ	NOVEMBER ՆՈԵՄԲԵՐ	DECEMBER ԴԵԿՏԵՄԲԵՐ
1	we 1 չրք	sa 1 շբթ	mo 1 երկ	th 1 հնգ	sa 1 շբթ
2 երկ	th 2 հնգ	2 կիր	2 երք	fr 2 ուր	2 կիր
3 երք	fr 3 ուր	mo 3 երկ	we 3 չրք	3 շբթ	mo 3 երկ
4 չրք	sa 4 շբթ	tu 4 երք	th 4 հնգ	4 կիր	tu 4 երք
5 հնգ	5 կիր	we 5 չրք	fr 5 ուր	mo 5 երկ	we 5 չրք
6 ուր	mo 6 երկ	th 6 հնգ	sa 6 շբթ	tu 6 երք	th 6 հնգ
7 շբթ	7 երք	7 ուր	7 կիր	7 չրք	7 ուր
8	we 8 չրք	sa 8 շբթ	mo 8 երկ	th 8 հնգ	sa 8 շբթ
9	th 9 հնգ	9 կիր	tu 9 երք	fr 9 ուր	9 կիր
10 երք	10 ուր	mo 10 երկ	we 10 չրք	sa 10 շբթ	10 երկ
11 չրք	sa 11 շբթ	tu 11 երք	th 11 հնգ	11 կիր	tu 11 երք
12 հնգ	12 կիր	we 12 չրք	fr 12 ուր	12 երկ	we 12 չրք
13 ուր	mo 13 երկ	th 13 հնգ	sa 13 շբթ	tu 13 երք	13
14 շբթ	tu 14 երք	fr 14 ուր	14 կիր	we 14 չրք	14
15 կիր	15 ուր	15 շբթ	mo 15 երկ	th 15 հնգ	15
16 երկ	th 16 հնգ	16 կիր	tu 16 երք	fr 16 ուր	16
17 ուր	fr 17 ուր	mo 17 երկ	we 17 չրք	sa 17 շբթ	17
18 ջրբ	18 շբթ	tu 18 երք	th 18 հնգ	18 կիր	18
19 հնգ	19 կիր	we 19 չրք	fr 19 ուր	mo 19 երկ	19
20 ուր	mo 20 երկ	20 հնգ	sa 20 շբթ	20 երկ	20
21 զրբ	tu 21 երք	fr 21 ուր	21 կիր	we 21 ուր	21
22	we 22 չրք	sa 22 շբթ	mo 22 երկ	th 22 հնգ	22
23 հնգ	23	23 կիր	23 երք	fr 23	23

WHITE ON WHITEBOARD CALENDAR 2012

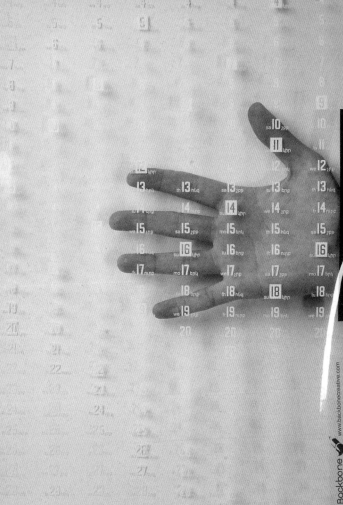

www.backbonecreative.com

Design by **Backbone** CREATIVE STUDIO

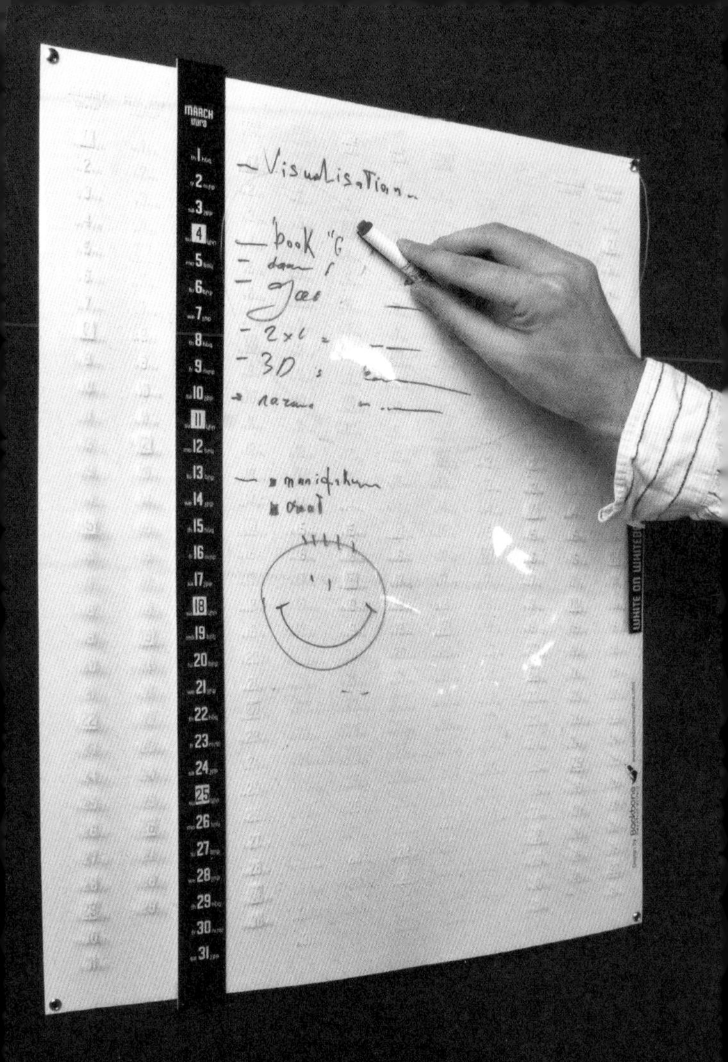
MARCH
Visualisation
WHITE ON WHITE

"Transparency shows everything. It gives an apparent access but never a sense of closeness."

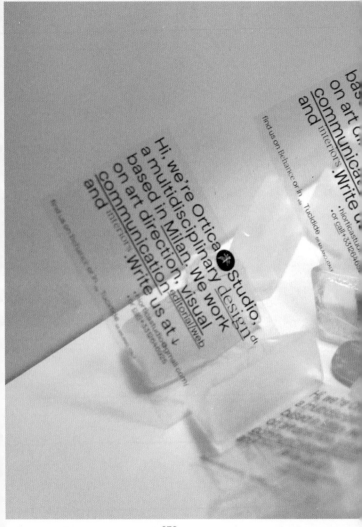

Hi, we're Ortica Studio, design dir a multidisciplinary design. We work based in Milan. visual on art direction. communication .Write us at ↓ and interiors editorial/web

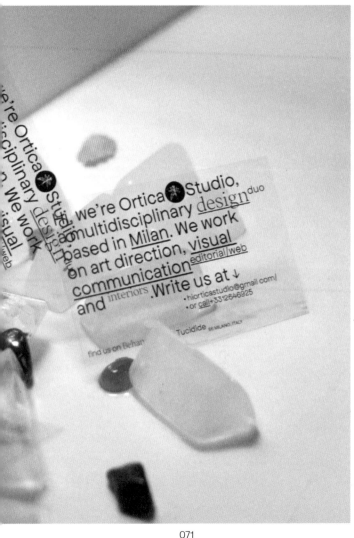

Hi, we're Ortica ✳ Studio, a multidisciplinary design^duo based in Milan. We work on art direction, visual communication^editorial/web and interiors. Write us at ↓
• hiorticastudio@gmail.com/
• or call +3312646925

Tucidide 69 MILANO, ITALY

find us on Behance

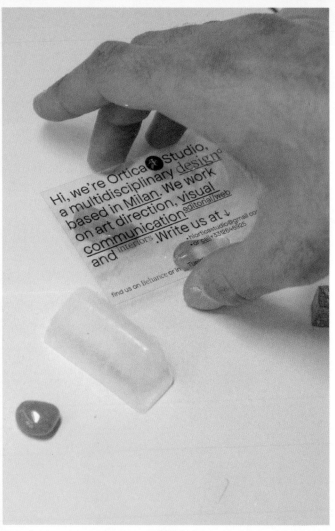

Hi, we're Ortica ✳ studio,
a multidisciplinary design°
based in Milan. We work
on art direction, visual
communication editorial/web
and interiors. Write us at ↓
• hiorticastudio@gmail.com
• or call +33126-45925

find us on Behance or in ... Tueb...

Hi, we're Ortica Studio, a multidisciplinary design duo based in Milan. We work on art direction, visual communication editorial/web and interiors. Write us at ↓
- • hiorticastudio@gmail com/
- • or call +33126+6925

find us on Behance or in via Tucidide 56 MILANO, ITALY

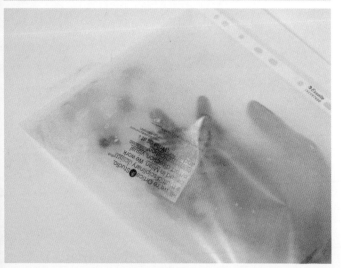

Hi, we're Ortica Studio,
a multidisciplinary design
based in Milan. We work
on art direction, visual
communication and
more.

N I S B I T T E
B O G M E F E V
D E W O O R E T
L E S S O I Y O
S E S D H N F
Y N I B W E T V
O G U T I W I A
U T N B F S H K
H R S E L A L E
E N Y D A E R N

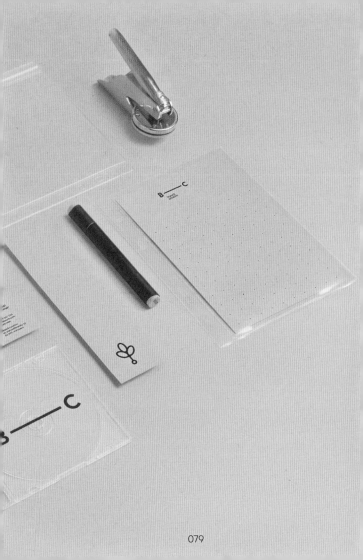

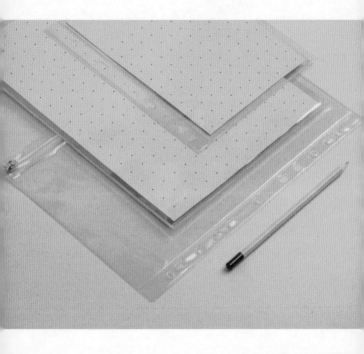

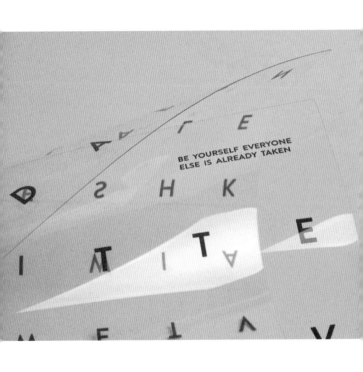

BE YOURSELF EVERYONE
ELSE IS ALREADY TAKEN

aether

Aether can be
using this as our
o   it forms ideas, c

Graphics
Branding
Art direction
Typography
Webdesign

3

1°09'18.2"N 41°05'5"E

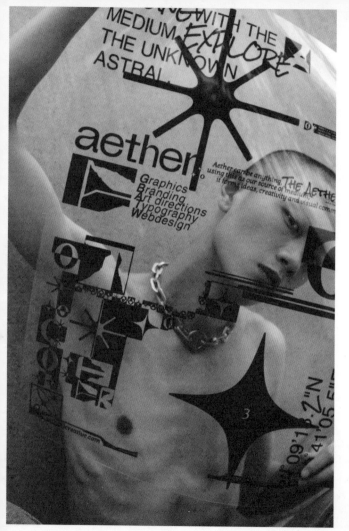

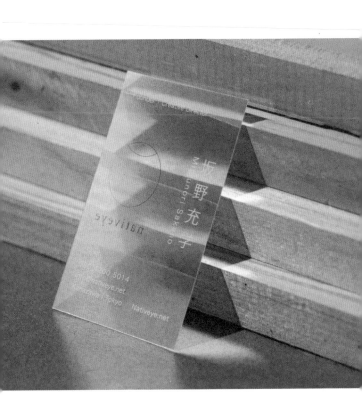

Founder & Creative Director

坂野充学

Mitsunori Sakano

nativeeye

080 4200 5014

info@nativeeye.net

Kanazawa Tokyo Nativeye.net

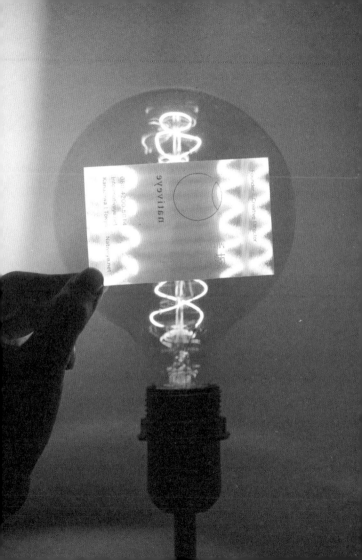

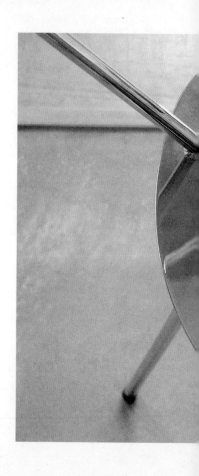

"Your library is your portrait." ———— Holbrook Jackson

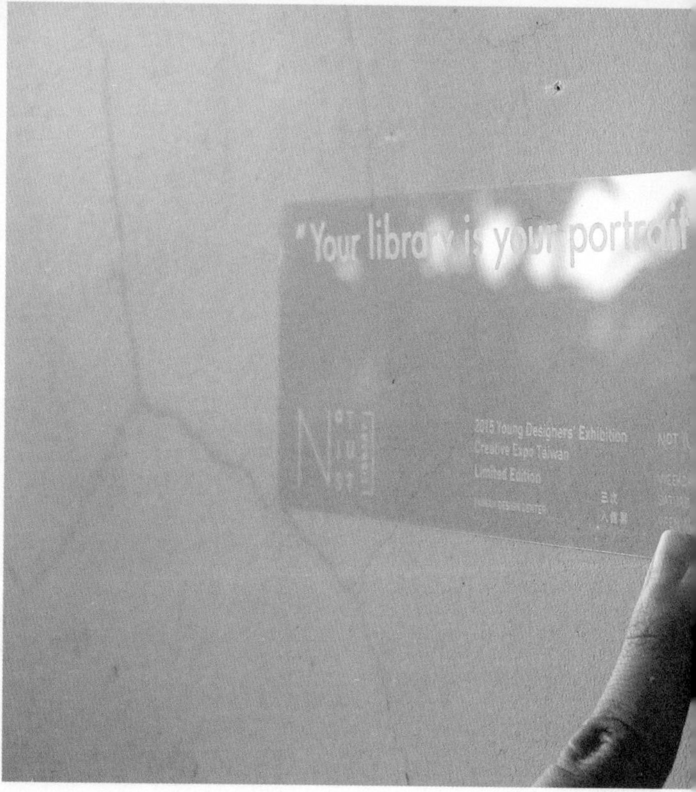
"Your library is your portrai
2015 Young Designers' Exhibition
Creative Expo Taiwan
Limited Edition

You And The Music
COMPILED BY DJ KAWASAKI

01. Where Would We Go
   feat. Paul Randolph & MAKOTO / DJ KAWASAKI
02. We Are On The Move feat. Eric Roberson / 2u!
03. Stand Up (with Pete Simpson) / Lay-Far
04. Girl I'm Running Back 2 U feat. Christian Urich
   (MAKOTO 4X4 ReBit) / MAKOTO
05. Boogie (Original Mix) / Uptown Funk Empire
06. Breaking Bad / Art Of Tones
07. Still Running (My Heart) / E.D.O
08. Can't Stop (Original Mix) / Cweatlife
09. All The Right / Wagon Cookin' feat. Gabriela Smith
10. All Night (Everybody) / Kon feat. Amy Douglas
11. Get Yourself Together
   (Timmy's B'ham Disco Authority Mix)
   / Timmy Vegas feat. Kony Davies
12. Stop The World (Tanztubar Club Mix)
   / Tanztubar feat. Renn
13. The Party After (Reel People Remix) / Mutant

You And The Music
Compiled by DJ KAWASAKI Release Tour

7/19(sat)   渋谷 The Room
7/26(sat)   札幌 ACID ROOM
8/9(sat)   京都 MUSIC BAR COLORS
8/30(sat)   熊本 2115 (two one one zero)
9/22(mon-祝日) 大分 Freedom
10/11(sat) 宇都宮 SPACE LAB ₊
and more !

SELEC-10007
℗&© 2014 SELECTARE RECORDS
企画構成:選択
発売元:SELECTARE RECORDS
販売元:BBQ CO.,LTD.
Printed in Japan / STEREO
24・8・8・8(ホール)DP有

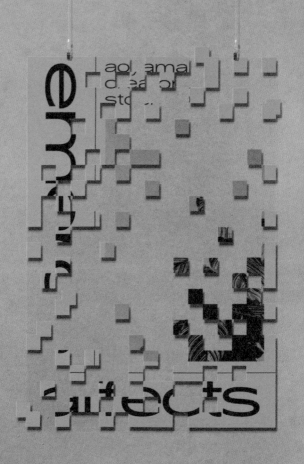

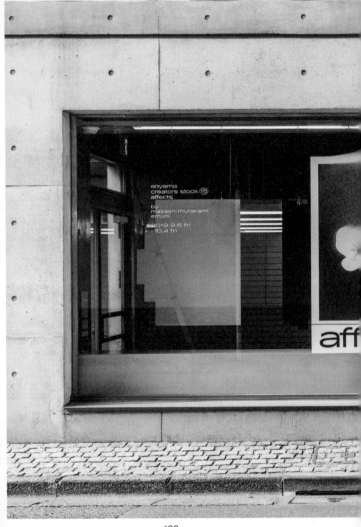

"Transparency is powerful for physical communications like direct mail."

PATTERN
ON
PATTERN

L FORET

PRIVATE

PA RTY

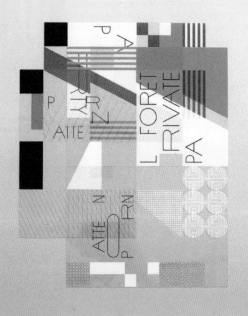

PA

PRIVATE

L FORET

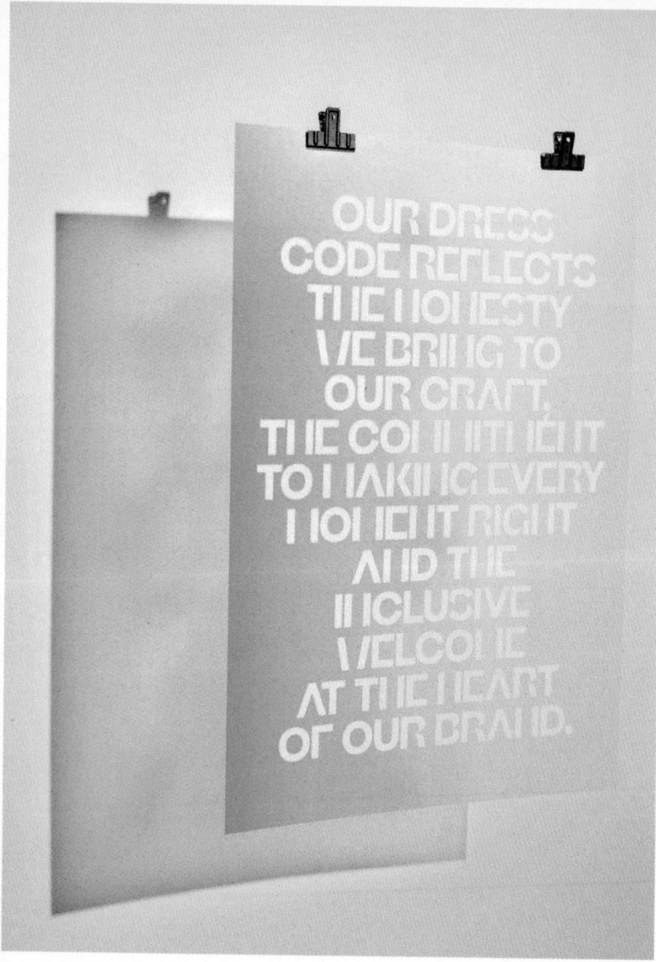

OUR DRESS
CODE REFLECTS
THE HONESTY
WE BRING TO
OUR CRAFT,
THE COMMITMENT
TO MAKING EVERY
MOMENT RIGHT
AND THE
INCLUSIVE
WELCOME
AT THE HEART
OF OUR BRAND.

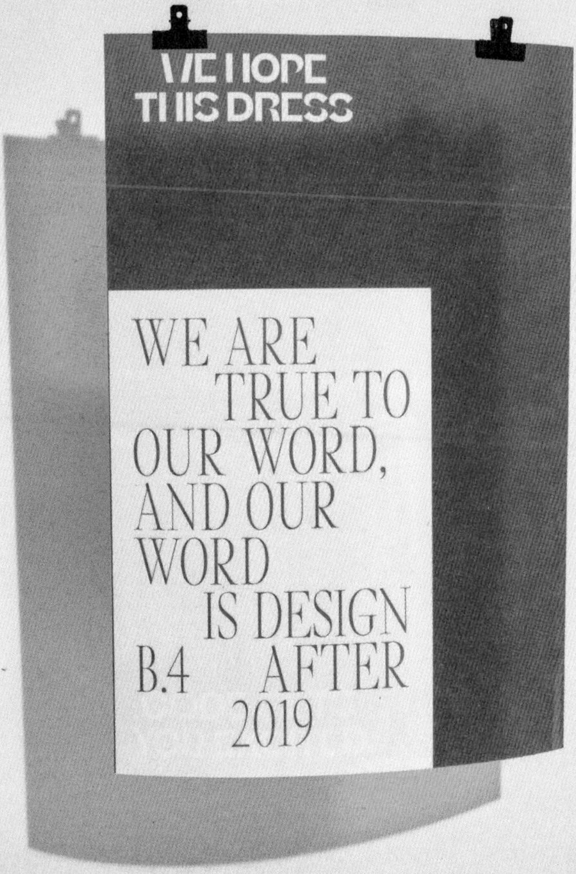

WE HOPE
THIS DRESS

WE ARE
　　TRUE TO
OUR WORD,
AND OUR
WORD
　　IS DESIGN
B.4　　AFTER
　　2019

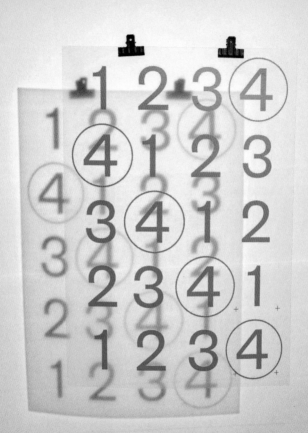

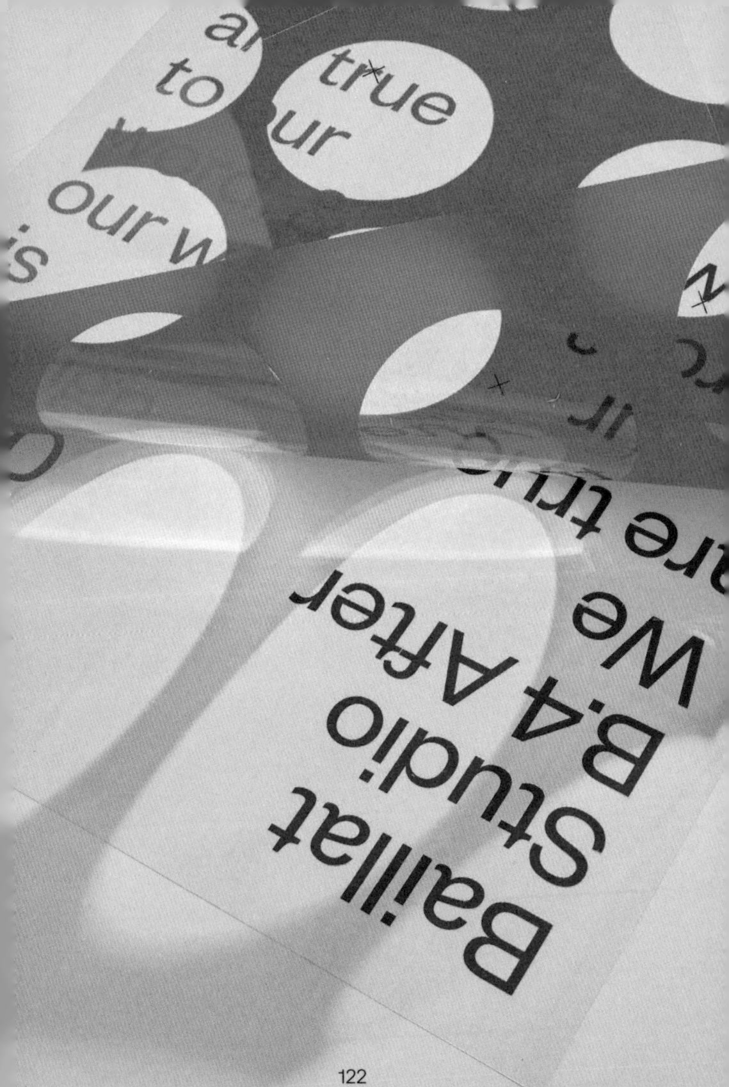
to
true
our w
Baillat
Studio
B.4 After
We
re tru

123

...ctuous
...ave yet pleasant
...orruptible
...all dresses may be critical
...ckets may be biased
...nts may be equivocating
...es may be presentable
...d and silver chains may be skepti
...elets of ivory may be moral
...en and jewelled belts may be
...ng

...s of amber may be splendid
...may be polished
...es and buckles may be c
...s may be divine
...y be excellent
...s may be civilized
...may be well formed
...may be awe-inspiring
...y be fearsome
...of embroidery may be o
...ay be refined
...be majestic
...e mind-blowing
...ay be unforeseen
...y dresses will fight the B
...l fight the Unsurprisin
...s and tweed blaze
...ual
...kle boots will fig
...coats will fight
...fun blouses will fight
...nd collared shirt will
...t the Predictable
...tretchy-fabric
...l fight the
...that drag on t
...eary
...notono

C201917:00

Our
Our b
Our be
Our ne
Our colo
...d p
...gh
...aotr
...colo
...le pat
...gh
...d or distra
...ural enough
...hall or modere
...e genuine enoug
...nose studs shall b
...enough
...body ornaments sha
...ough
...studs shall be
...esigns will not b
...ard
...ttoos on face and
...sible tattoos will dazz
...achable
...will stay straight
...eoks will revolt
...shirts will reveal themselves
...securely fastened buttons or pins wi
...be dead serious.
...r buttons or pins that vocate a political
...religious or personal issue will be
...self-composed

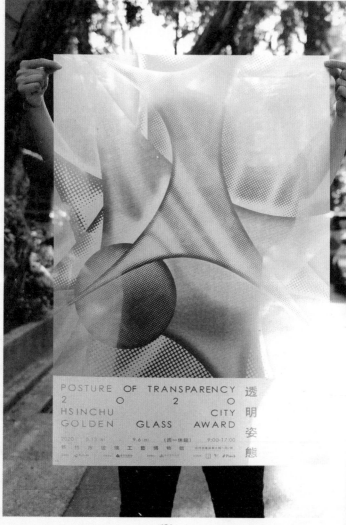

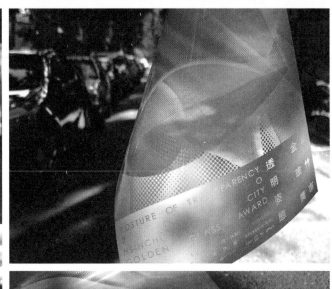

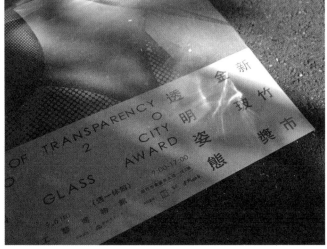

TRANSPARENCY
2
GLASS
O
CITY
AWARD
透
明
金
新
玻
竹

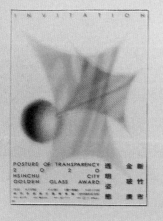

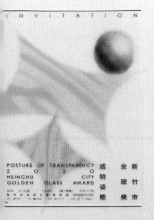

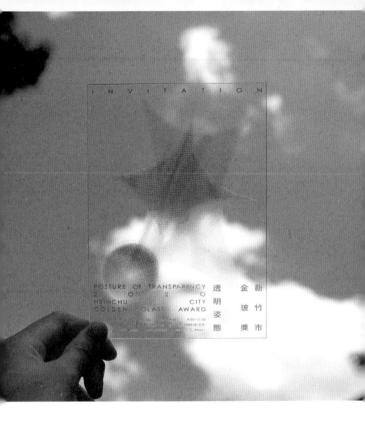

GOLDEN
GLASS
AWARD

新竹市
金玻獎
暨 文創設計工藝創作比賽

2020 HSINCHU CITY

GOLDEN
GLASS
AWARD

新竹市
玻璃獎

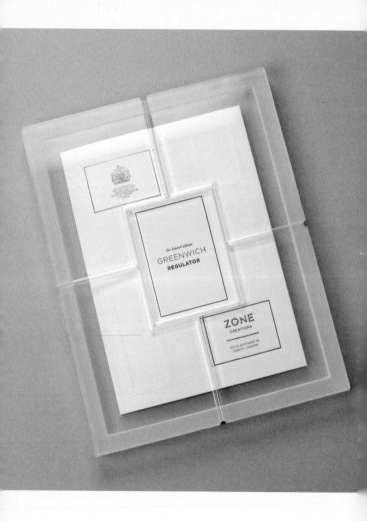

"Now, go away ... I want to go down from the wall!"

99

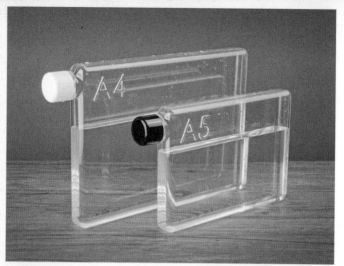

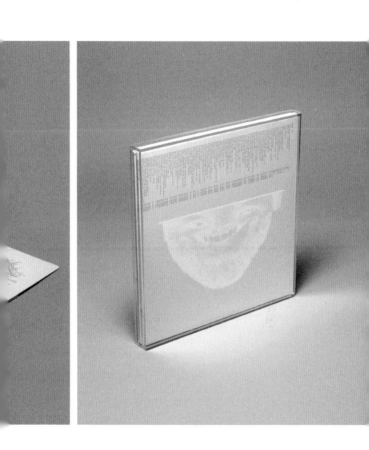

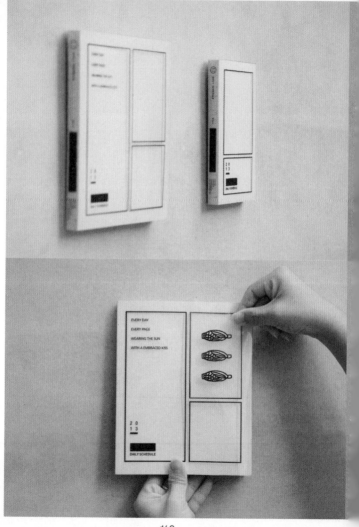

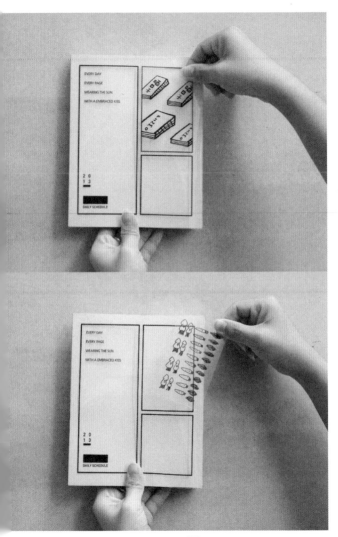

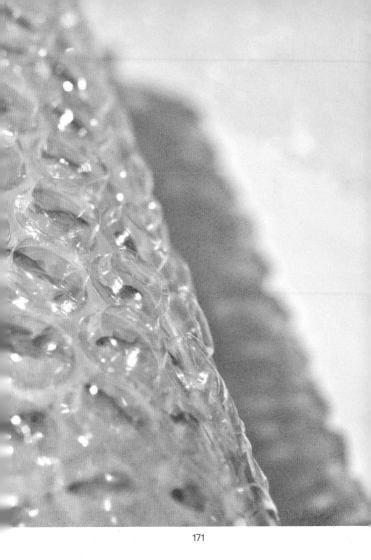

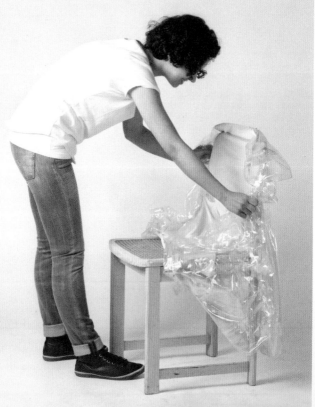

"With the vacuum bag, the couples embraced each other firmly and the degree of adhesion expresses the depth of love."

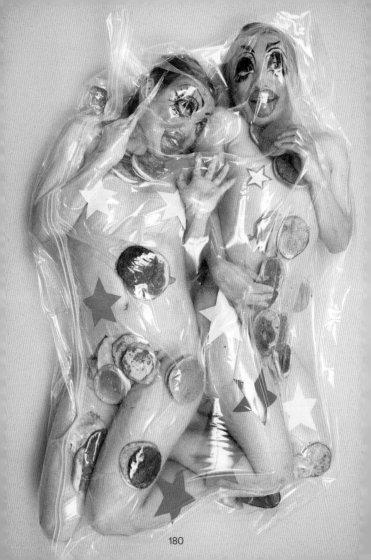

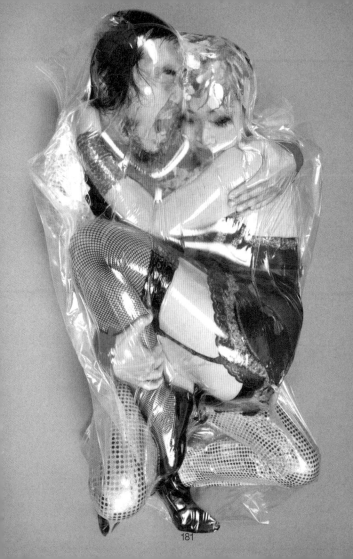

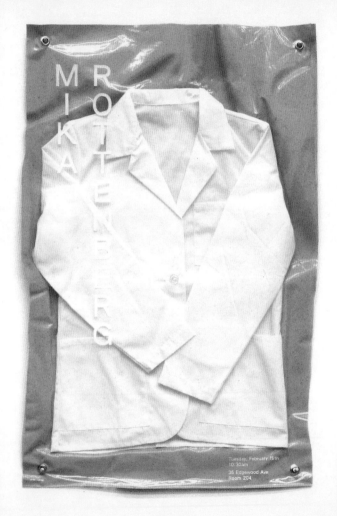

John
Mc in
Mery

Tuesday, February 26th
10.30 am
In Edgewood, Room 304

185

RASHID
JOHNSON

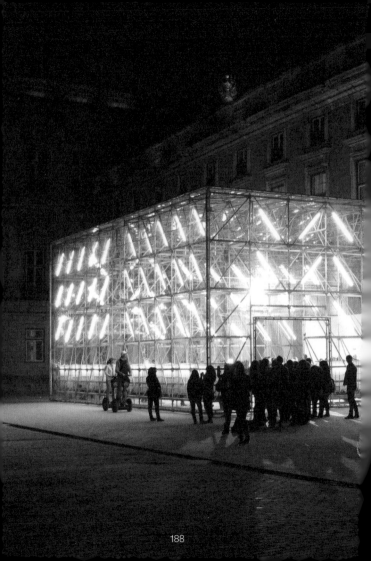

CLUB

CLUB

white christmas fair

2013.11.15.fri-

白のけはい

note et silex

2013.11.15.fri-

e christmas fair

e et silence.

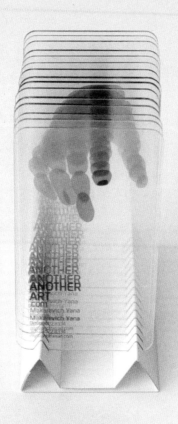

ANOTHER
ART
.com

Makarevich Yana
Designer

**ANOTHER
ART
.com**

From   Yana Makarevich
Designer

Street one Street
224000 Minsk, Belarus

+375 29 1228334
makarevich@anart.com

To   Valery Polschenko
Co-founder

30 Moskovskaya Street
224000 Minsk, Belarus

+375 29 5331245
valery@another.com

ANOTHER
ART
.com

Makarevich Yana
Designer

+375 29 5208304
makarevich@mail.com

ANOTHER
ART
.com

| From | What's new? | License agreement | From | Yana Makarevich |
| | | | | Designer |

MERRY CHRISTMAS
AND A HAPPY NEW YEAR

Services agreement RELATIONS

Personal notification

EUR 800.00

Makarevich Yana
Designer

Makarevich Yana
Designer

Makarevich Yana
Designer

EUR 1500.00

Makarevich Yana
Designer

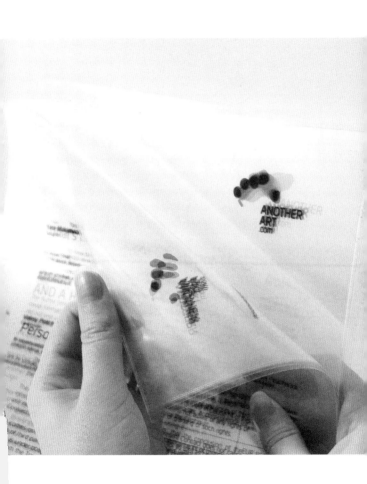

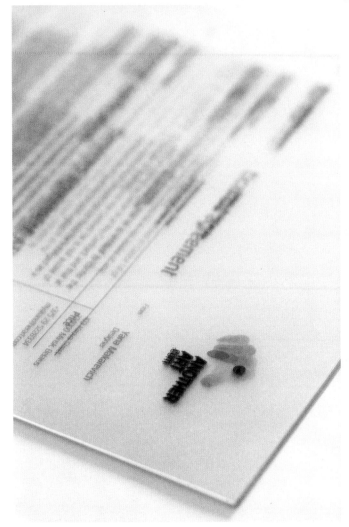

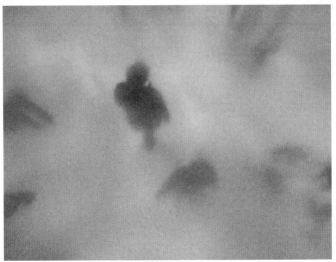

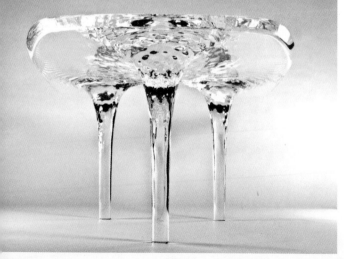

"There's a great depth in transparency as it is the representation of light. Transparent objects reveal themselves as light hits them, and transform as light dances."

229

246

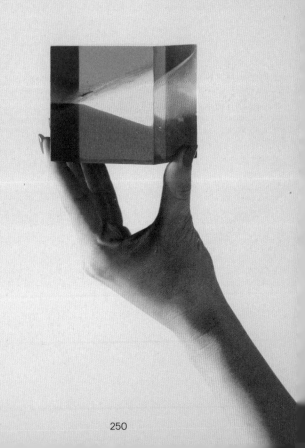

265

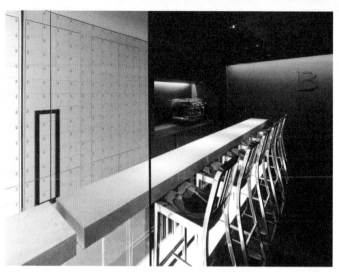

267

"Life is like a
box of chocolates.
You never know what
you're gonna get."

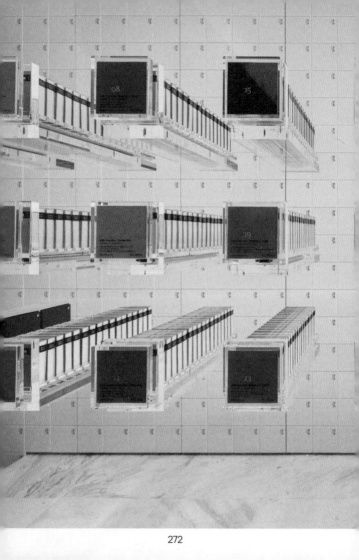

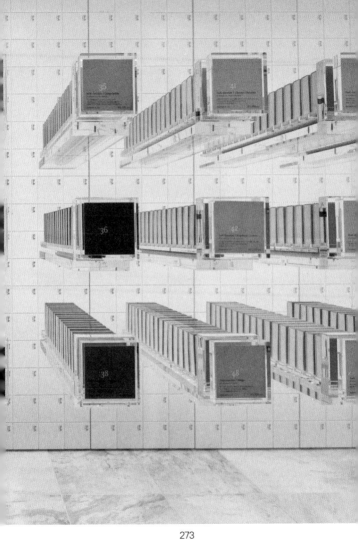

PREMIS
INNOVACAT
2014
AVANÇA

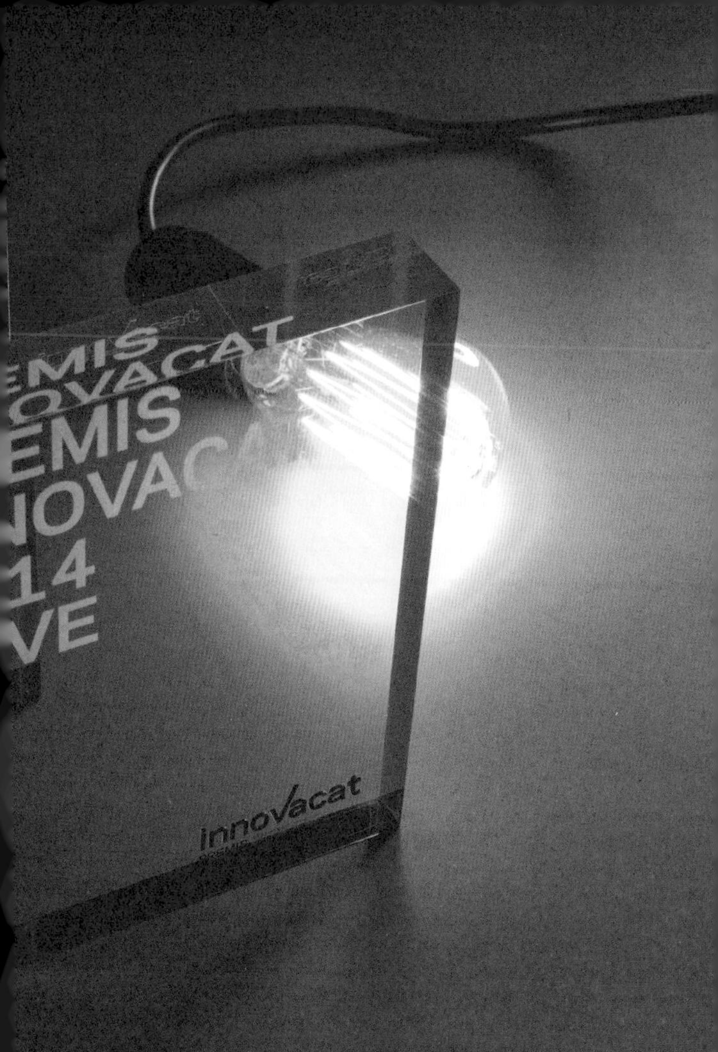
innoVacat

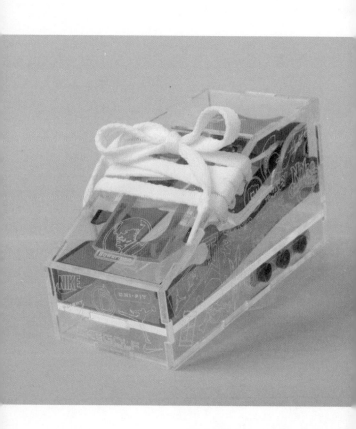

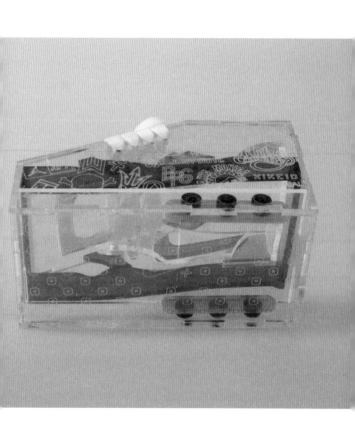

Exploring the Creative Overlap

293

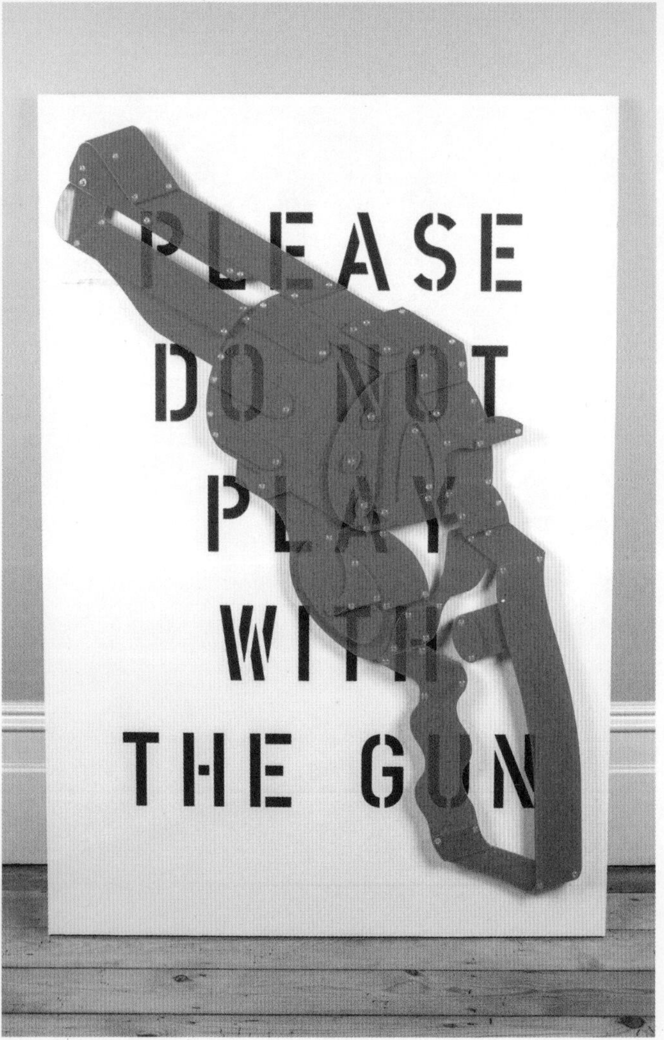
PLEASE
DO NOT
PLAY
WITH
THE GUN

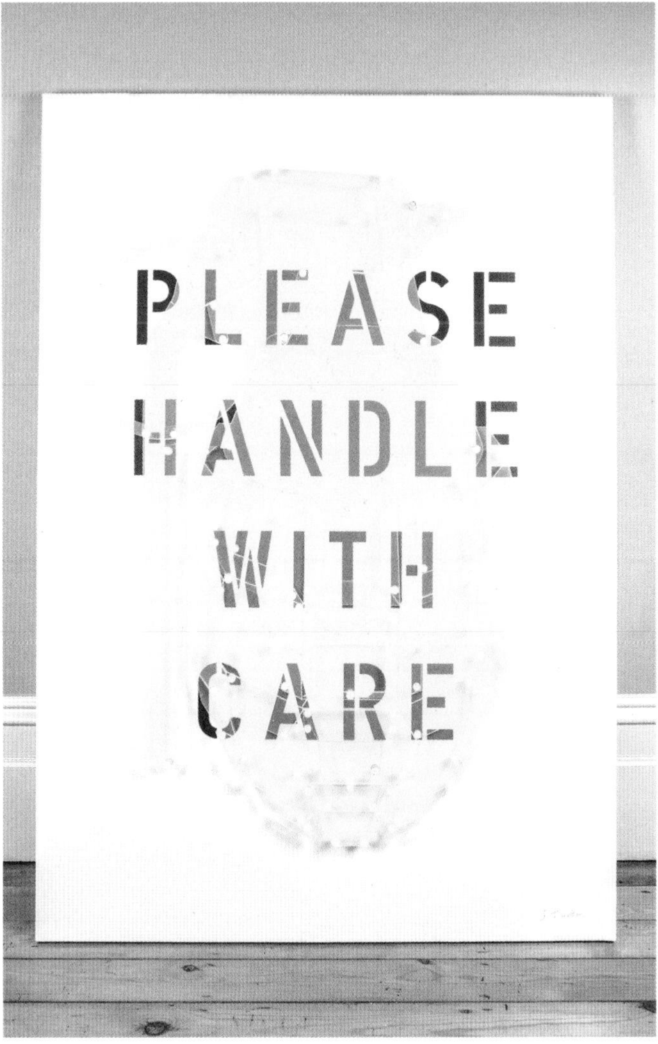
PLEASE
HANDLE
WITH
CARE

Que signifie le rire? Qu'y a-t-il au fond du risible? Que trouverait-on de si commun entre une grimace de pitre, un jeu de mots, un quiproquo de vaudeville, une scène de fine comédie? Quelle distillation nous donnera l'essence, toujours la même, à laquelle tant de produits divers empruntent ou leur indiscrète odeur ou leur parfum délicat? Les plus grands penseurs, depuis Aristote, se sont attaqués à ce petit problème, qui toujours se dérobe sous l'effort, glisse, s'échappe, se re-

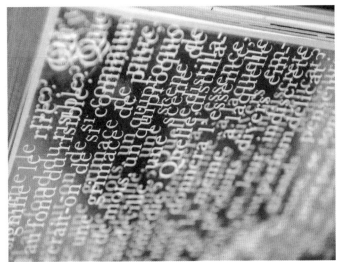

"Colour is ordinarily the defining feature of products. By removing this distinctive characteristic we bring out their texture and re-emphasise their essential aspects."

eautiful
ind

MATHIEU LEHANNEUR

David Edwards of Le Laboratoire draws fresh inspiration from a Mathieu Lehanneur think-tank based on the human brain.

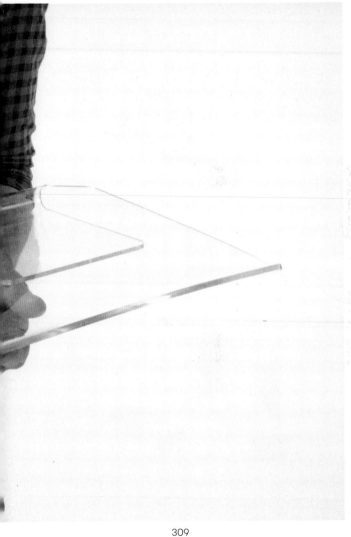

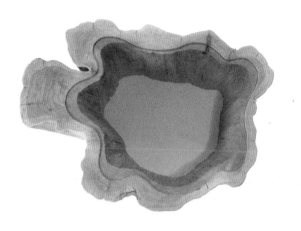

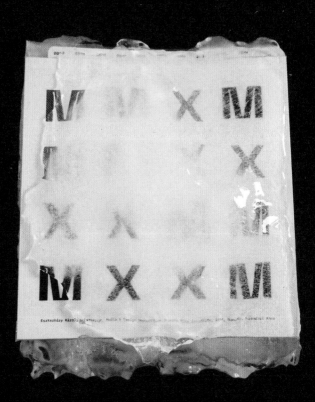

Esterházy Károly [...] [...]

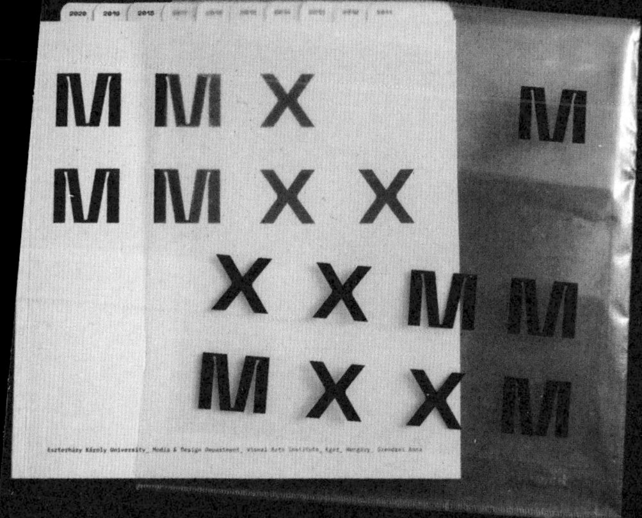
2020
2019
2018
Eszterházy Károly University_ Media & Design

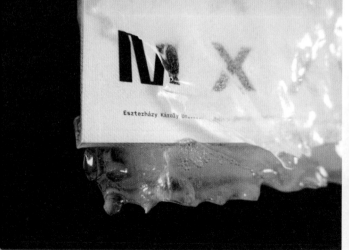

Beatific™
Youth Elixir
face serum

Beatific™
Extreme Anti-Aging
face cream

Beatific™
Instant Beauty Booster
face mask

Beatific™
Hydrating Comfort
serum

Beatific™
Instant Beauty Booster
face mask

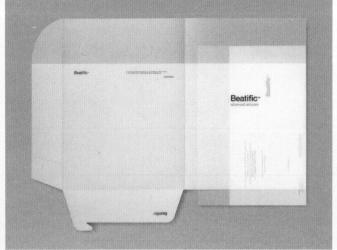

Doctors' way
to beauty miracles

Beatific™

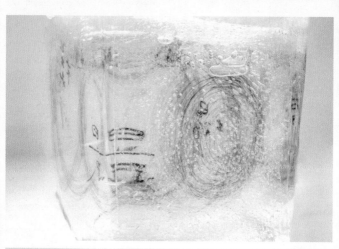

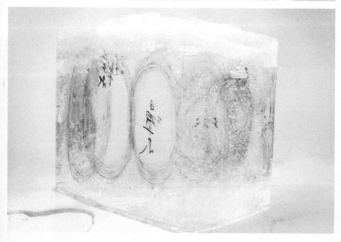

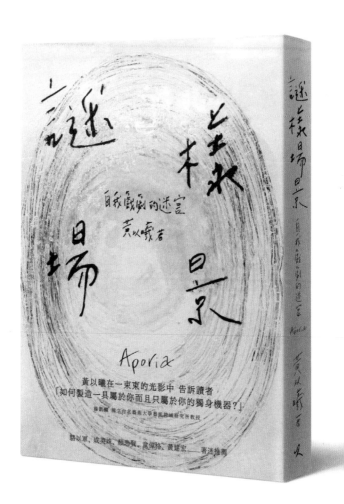

謎樣日常

自我戲劇的迷宮

黃以曦 著

Aporia

黃以曦在一束束的光影中 告訴讀者

「如何製造一具屬於你面且只屬於你的獨身機器？」

楊凱麟 國立臺北藝術大學藝術跨域研究所教授

駱以軍、成英姝、顏忠賢、黃俊搞、黃建宏──著迷推薦

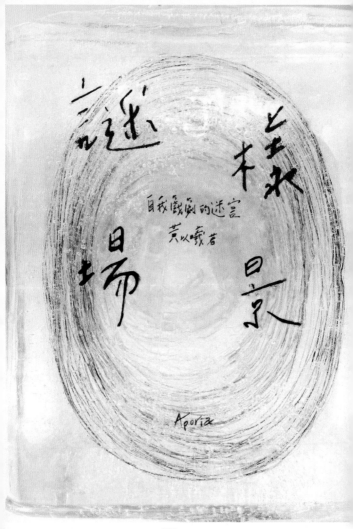

謎樣劇場

自我戲劇的迷宮

黃以曦 著

Aporia

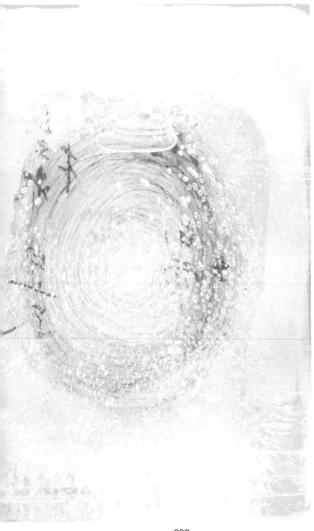

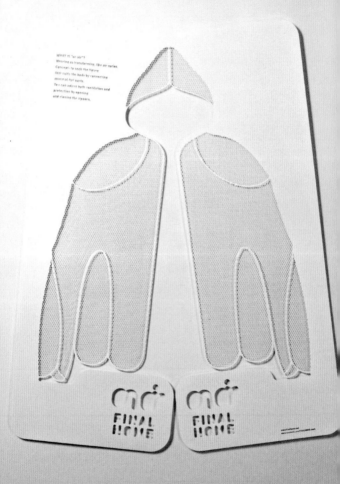

WHAT IS "en air"?
Wearing as transforming, like air varies.
Concept: to seek the figure
that suits the body by connecting
minimal flat parts.
You can adjust both ventilation and
protection by opening
and closing the zippers.

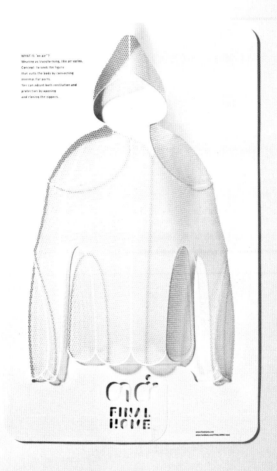

FINAL
HOME

www.finalhome.com
www.facebook.com/FINAL.HOME.news

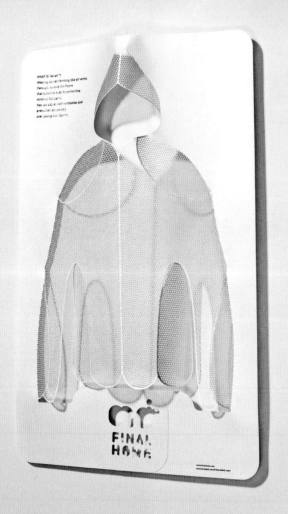

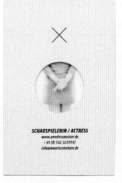

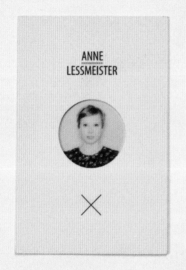

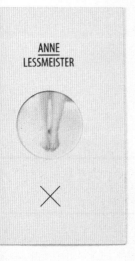

ANNE
LESSMEISTER

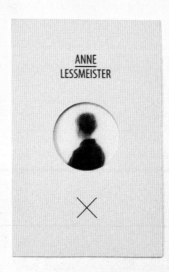

ANNE
LESSMEISTER

THE
END
AGE

"Transparency is used to give an ethereal sensation by the eyes, that influences the taste."

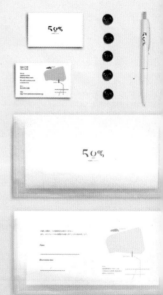

50%

MENU

サラダ/ 氷の下の小魚 // salad
// little fishes under the ice .... 750 ¥
// flower garden and white fish .... 750 ¥
ル お肉 // March hydrangea .... 750 ¥
少女の階段 // Main dish .... 750 ¥
晶晶 // stair of the girl .... 750 ¥
コーヒー // glitter .... 750 ¥
.... 750 ¥

Coffee

.... 750 ¥

361

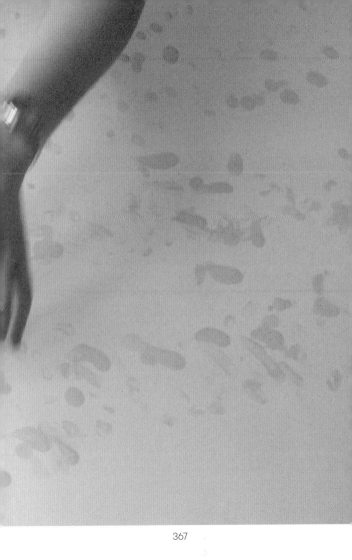

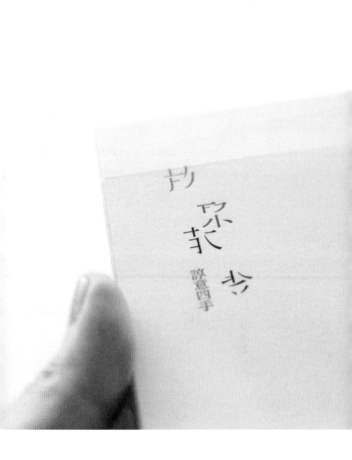

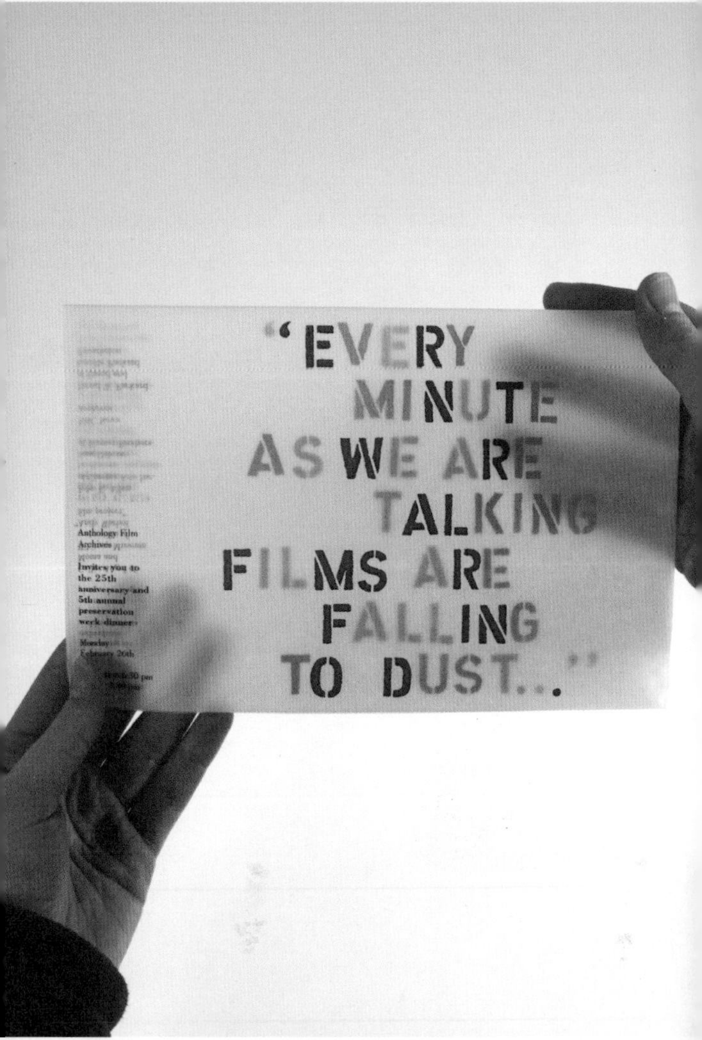

"EVERY
MINUTE
AS WE ARE
TALKING
FILMS ARE
FALLING
TO DUST..."

Anthology Film
Archives

invites you to
the 25th
anniversary and
5th annual
preservation
week dinner

Monday,
February 26th

6:00-6:30 pm
7:00 pm

Anthology Film
Archives

Invite you to
the 25th
anniversary and
5th annual
preservation
week dinner

Monday
February 26th
2001
Reception 6:30 pm
Dinner 7:30 pm

Honorary chairman
Martin Scorsese

Honoring six
individuals
and institutions
preserving
our motion
picture heritage:

Callie Angel of
Menu and
Whitney Museum
restoration of
"Andy Warhol
film project"

John E. Allen
of Cinema Arts Inc.

Sam Gelvanic
of Warner Brothers

NBC News
Archives

David W. Packard
of David and
Lucille Packard
Foundation

The 5th annual
preservation week
provides also
projections and
lectures at
the Anthology Film
Archives Theatre
at 80, Mercator st.

Call Anthology
Film Archives for a
catalogue of the
programme and more
information:
212. 505 5181
fax 212. 477 2714

371

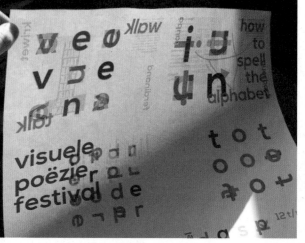

374

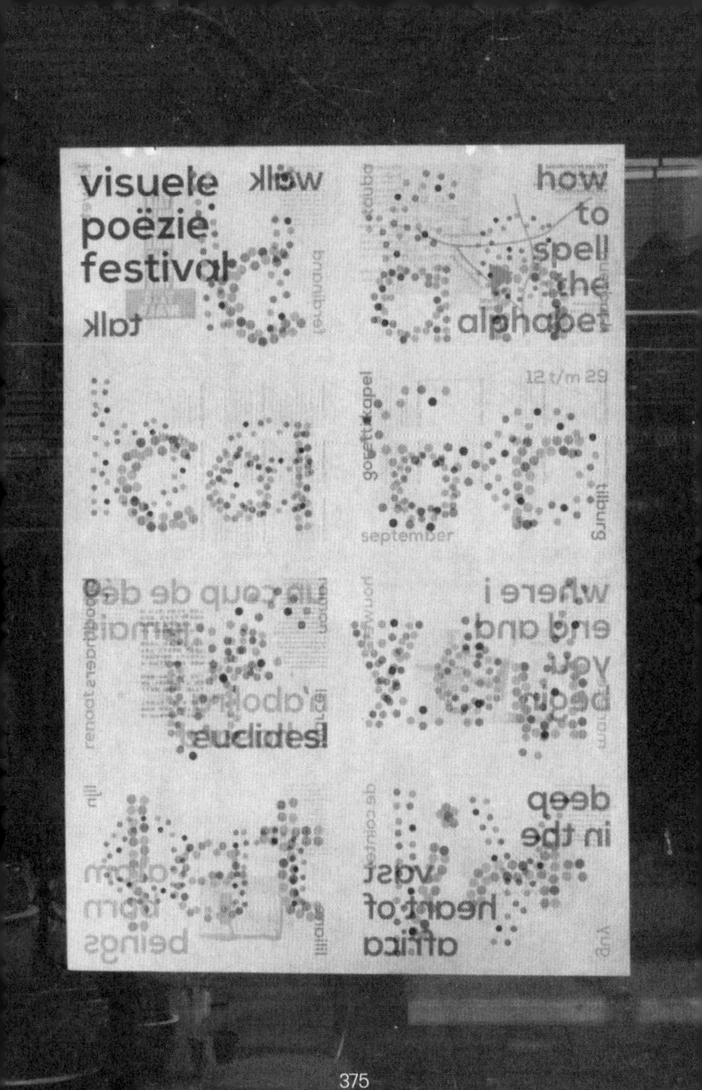
visuele
poëzie
festival
how
to
spell
the
alphabet
12 t/m 29
september
tilburg
where i
end and
you
begin
un coup de dés
jamais
d'abolir
euclides!
deep
in the
vast
heart of
africa

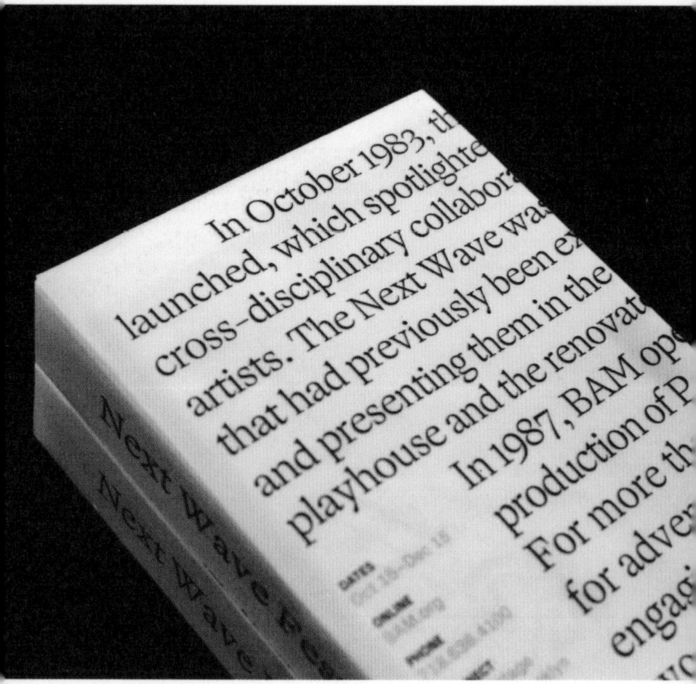

In October 1983, th
launched, which spotlighte
cross-disciplinary collabora
artists. The Next Wave wa
that had previously been e
and presenting them in the
playhouse and the renovat

In 1987, BAM op
production of P
For more th
for adver
engagi

Next Wave Fe
Next Wave Fe

DATES Oct 15–Dec 15

ONLINE BAM.org

PHONE 718.636.4100

Two audiences one starts at the BAM Fisher, the other at BAM Rose Cinemas. Both see the same performance, through two very different lenses: theater, film, created by

02

The

October 18–1...

Inoa...

October 23–27

04

What if they wer...
Moscow? October...

User N...

These
supplying, pro...
original way. They A...
In a different way. A...
been to Next Wave...
to introduce you to the...
You're joining us to...
excited to build to...

Swan Lake /
och na hEala

01

d Woman

3

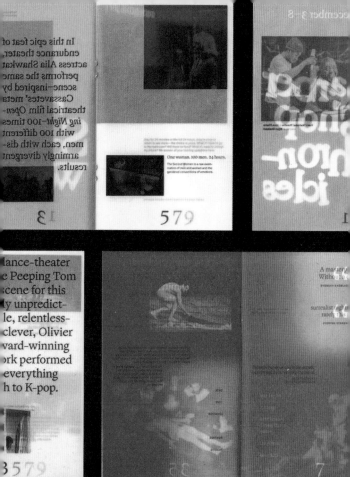

In this epic feat of endurance theater, actress Alia Shawkat performs the same scene—inspired by Cassavetes' meta theatrical film Open-ing Night 100 times with 100 different men, each with dis-armingly divergent results.

13

One woman. 100 men. 24 hours.

The Second Woman is a rare exam-ination of men and women and the gendered connections of emotions.

579

dance-theater e Peeping Tom scene for this ly unpredict-le, relentless-clever, Olivier ward-winning rk performed everything h to K-pop.

3579

A matter Without

surrealist rarely

7

Set inside bar-
ber shops in six
different cities,
playwright Inua
Ellams weaves
...ch, joyful tapestry
...nfiltered stories
...ut father-son re-
...onships and black
...sculinity, set to
...Afrobeat score.

Bear witness via sma...
a stranger's profound...
experience in this sit...
play, which contemp...
afterlife on the intern...
and our shifting notio...
of connection.

What happens to your digital
life after you're gone?

Mad, subversive, anti-
festive brilliance...
Describing it doesn't do it
justice. Go and see it

TIME OUT LONDON

Searingly funny and
heartbreaking... Meow Meow
is one Christmas present that
won't disappoint

LOS ANGELES TIMES

Dec 12–14

7.30pm

BAM Harvey
Theatre

TBD

All at $25

Come all ye seekers of yuletide delight
and mayhem the crowd-surfing Queen
of Chanson makes her BAM debut.

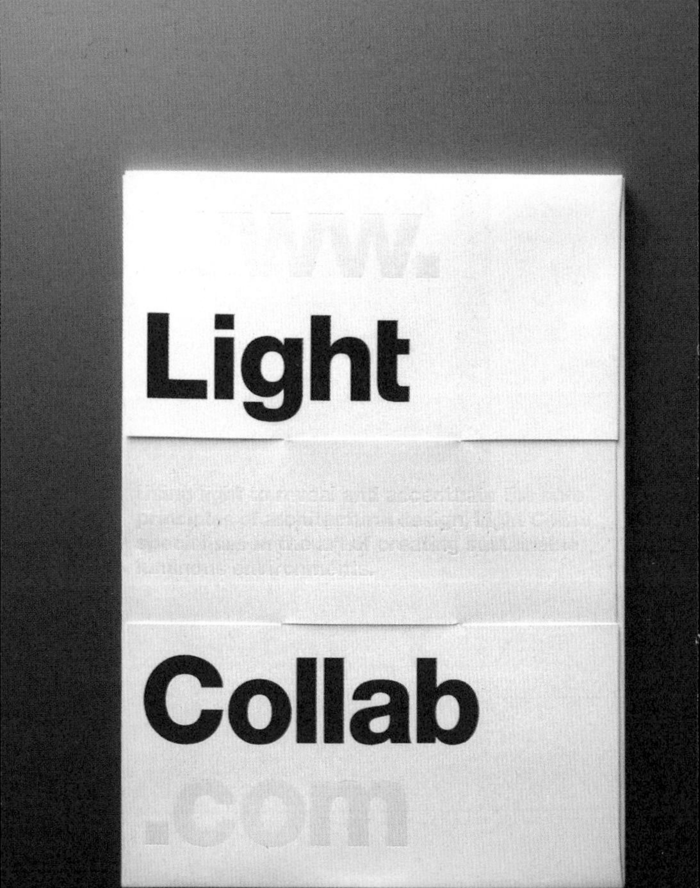
Light
Collab
.com

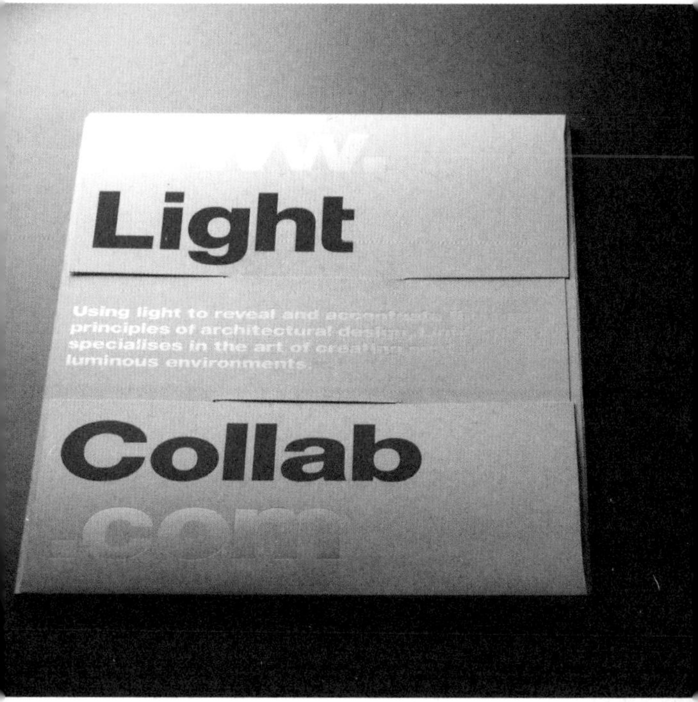
Light
Collab

Light

ing light to
rinciples of a
ecialises in
minous env

Colla

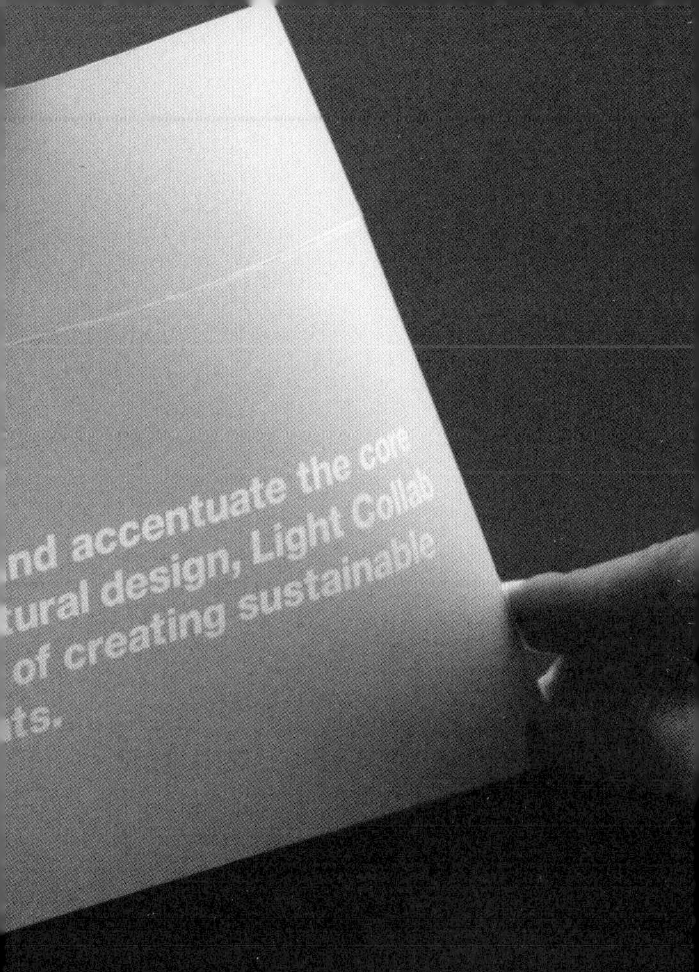

nd accentuate the core
tural design, Light Collab
of creating sustainable
ts.

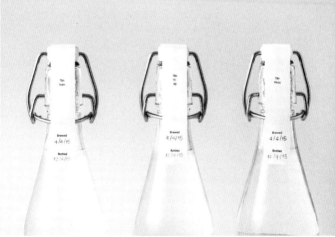

ice
wine

50

Pure hand-crafted
Vietnamese Rice Wine

Pure Bottled Ciou!
From the Central Highlands

CARE

活著

日其⋯⋯六月廿三日巳上席

若主　心月茶事

余文心　陳凱璇　周靜雯　黎文菁

劉淑儀　王俊文　楊曉豐

補助　陳美芝　陳鼎文

前席品目

盆栽　綠意盎然

主席品目

水注　市川孝　白釉燒水壺

茶心壺　琉璃光罐子

茗甌　紅寶琉璃碗子

茶　莚山綠茶

茶服　粉白素色

摩夏月發尼翔暈禱者

ABOVE OF TEA: SUMMER SOLSTICE TEA EVENT
ADDRESS: One Tea Room, 10F, 7 Mallory Street, Wan Chai, Hong Kong | 10600 Tealeet
TEA SERVING: Yu Man-sam, Pauline Chan, Jimmy Chau, Kelly Lau, Connie Liao, Lawrence Wong, Elton Young
TEA EXPERIENCE ASSISTANCE: Maggie Chan, Eva Chan

SESSION/DATE & TIME					
20 Jun (SAT)	20 Jun (SAT)	21 Jun (SUN)	21 Jun (SUN)	23 Jun (MON)	23 Jun (TUE)
11AM – 12:30PM	3:30PM – 4PM	11AM – 11:30PM	3:30PM – 4PM	11:30 – 4:30PM	3:30PM – 8:30PM

SESSION: Greenery
TEA KETTLE: Ceramic white ceramic pot by Takashi Ichikawa
TEA CADDY: Crystal glass tea caddy
TEA BOWL: Handmade glass by Rudy Woo
TEA LEAVES: Jip Mountain Green Tea 2020
TEA APPLICABLE: cozrinum, blanc de chao white

TEA ROOM DESIGN: MJRL Design
TEA MENU DESIGN: CoDesign Ltd.
GLASS STYLE: Ruby Woo
CALLIGRAPHER: Kit Xing Tio
WRITER: Yiu Man-sum

一碗茶

簡茶道下尋見自己

輕簡繁複的器具

解開形式的約束

徹底放棄多餘的干擾因素

屏蔽地方文化的線條屬性

眼前存在的

只有茶葉　水和嘗卜

熱水傾注　茶葉翻飛

有形與無形間

一呼一吸間

身心浸潤在

須臾的自在空間裡

飲茶　飲境　飲意

飲茶的境界

在意的僅是身象與感受

當心頃於茶意時

BEGINNING FROM A
SIMPLE BOWL OF TEA'
EXPERIENCE

Under the simple way of tea, meet yourself

Cut the frills to the ware

abandon constraints on form

let go of all unwanted distractions

omit the lines, their attributes and local cultures

all there are in sight

but the tea leaves and water, and the present

Between the someone and the abstract

hot water streams down, the leaves twirl

Between each breath

the body and mind natives

in a free and fleeting space

Tea, the surroundings and the ambiance

that's the way of tea, at focuses on walking

but where you are and how you feel

And as you pour yourself into it

all that in the world becomes beautiful.

398

設計　香港潮行茶藝雅集　羅佳文號王樹　番生

日期　二零二零年六月廿三日　上午席和下午席

茶主　心月茶事

協助　余文心　陳凱琪　同靜雯　蔡文菁
　　　劉淑儀　王俊文　楊曉豐
　　　陳美芝　陳鼎文

前席品目　綠意盎照

盆栽

水注　市川巽　自釉燒水壺

主席品目

茶心壺　琉璃光罐子

茗甌　紅寶琉璃碗子

茶　徑山綠茶

茶服　粉白素色

摩夏月慶鼠稣暑持香

A BOWL OF TEA | SUMMER SOLSTICE TEA EVENT

ADDRESS: One Tea Room, 3/F, 7 Mallory Street, Wan Chai, Hong Kong | HOST: Tenten
TEA SPECIALITY: Yu Man-sum, Frivin Chan, Jennie Chan, Kelly Lai, Grace Lui, Lawrence Wong, Eman Yeung
TEA EXPERIENCE AMBIANCE: Maggie Chan, Fee Chan

WORKSHOP DATE & TIME:

20 Jun (SAT)	30 Jun (SAT)	31 Jun (SUN)	21 Jun (SUN)	22 Jun (MON)	23 Jun (TUE)
11:2AM – 12:30PM	2:30PM – 4PM	11:2AM – 12:30PM	2:30PM – 4PM	7:15PM – 8:30PM	7:15PM – 8:30PM

MENU CATEGORY
TEA KETTLE: Creamy white ceramic pot by Takashi Ichikawa
TEA CADDY: Crystal glass tea caddy
TEA WARE: Handmade glass by Ruby Woo
TEA LEAVES: Jin Mountain Green Tea 2020
TEA SPECIALIST COSTUME: Blanc-de-chine white

TEA ROOM DESIGN: Milk Design
TEA MENU DESIGN: CoDesign Ltd.
GLASS ARTIST: Ruby Woo
CALLIGRAPHER: Xie Xing Tao
WRITER: Yu Man-sum

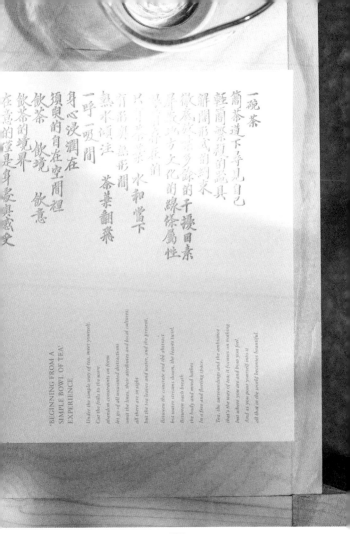

一碗茶

簡茶道下牽引自己
輕簡瑣碎的器具
解開形式的綑綁
微囊敗去多餘的干擾因素
屏棄地方文化的綠條屬性
眼下只有茶 水和當下

有形與無形間
熱水傾注 茶葉翻飛

一呼一吸間
身心浸潤在
須臾的自在空間裡
飲茶 飲境 飲意
飲茶的境界
在意的靈是身象與感受

BEGINNING FROM A
SIMPLE BOWL OF TEA
EXPERIENCE

Under the simple way of tea, wean yourself,
Cut the frills to the worn
abandon constraints on form
let go of all unwanted distractions
undo the lines, their attributes and local cultures
all there are in sight
but the tea leaves and water, and the present.

Between the concrete and the abstract
hot water streams down, the leaves twirl.
Between each breath
the body and mind bathes
In a free and fleeting space.

Tea, the surroundings and the ambiance
that's the way of tea; it focuses on nothing
but where you are and how you feel.
And as you pour yourself into it
all that in the world becomes beautiful.

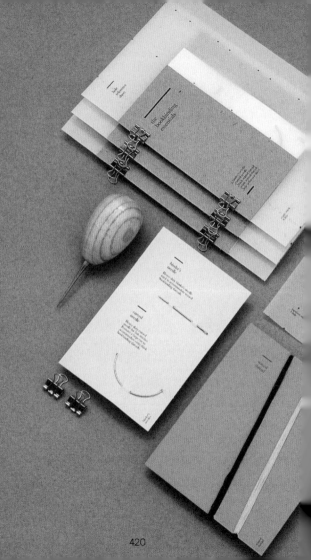

"The transparent cover creates an airy and light quality that nearly reserves itself to the background."

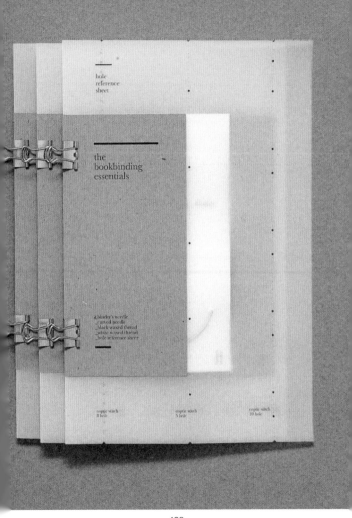

hole
reference
sheet

———

the
bookbinding
essentials

_binder's needle
_curved needle
_black waxed thread
_white waxed thread
_hole reference sheet

———

coptic stitch
8 hole

coptic stitch
5 hole

coptic stitch
10 hole

EN Lei, Felix / Hugh CHO / Yuh EGAMI / Baby×F
fung / LEUNG Kwok-shing / LI De / Joanne LI / LI
ic WONG / WONG Mei-yuk, Rebecca / WONG PIE-hu
& Becky Dance Group / City Contemporary Dance Com
ance Federation / La P en V Innovative Dance Platform
ENG / CHEUNG Fei-fan / CHONG Mui-ngam / CHU Pak-
du / Roy SZETO / Amy TAM / TO Kwok-wai, Raymond
/ Actors' Family / Alice Theatre Laboratory / Chung Yir
g Dramatists / Hong Kong Repertory Theatre / Hong Kr
heatre Workshop / Pants Theatre Production / Piece by
ers / The Radiant Theatre / Théâtre de la Feuille / The
ll Grass Theatre / Zuni

Explore Hong Kong
Performing Arts

e HO / Leon KO / KUNG

hung, Joyce / Alfred WONG / WONG Chi-wing, Cynthia
Die Konzertisten Charity Institute Limited / GDJYB / Ho
La Sax / Lo Tung Lo Percussion Group / Musica Viva
/ Yat Po Singers / CHENG Wing-mui, Susanna / KONG
an / YAU Sing-po / Johnson YUEN / Art of Cantonese
pera / Hong Kong Xiqu Troupe / Hong Kong Young Tal
am Sau Cantonese Opera Association / Ming Chee Sing
Music and Opera Association Limited / Shiny Light Trou
Kong / The Rainbow Fairy Cantonese Opera Laborator
ssociation / Wong Fai Puppet Shadow Company / Yeun
an NG / Contemporary Musiking Hong Kong / orleanla

HONG KONG AT CINARS 2018

427

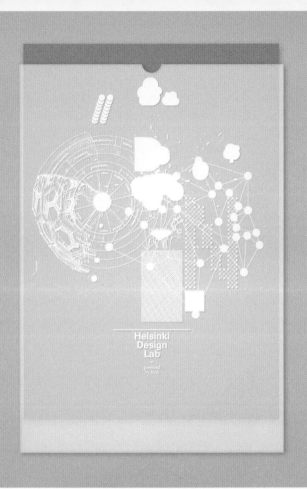

Helsinki
Design
Lab
—
powered
by SITRA

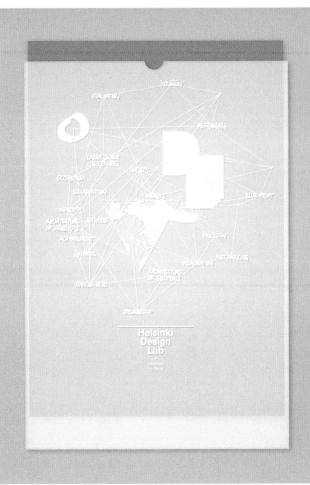

SUSTAINABILITY
EDUCATION
AGING

Helsinki
Design
Lab
—
powered
by Sitra

Helsinki
Design
Lab

—
powered
by Sitra

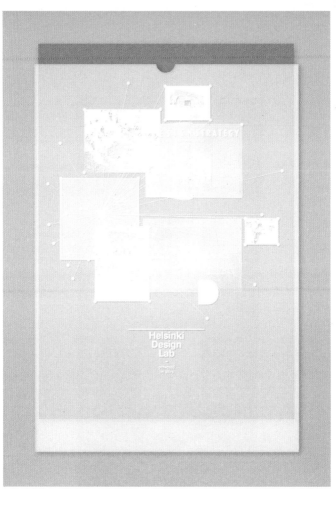

Helsinki
Design
Lab

powered
by sitra

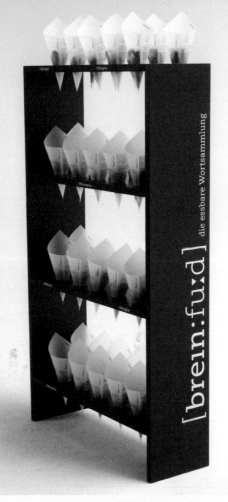

434

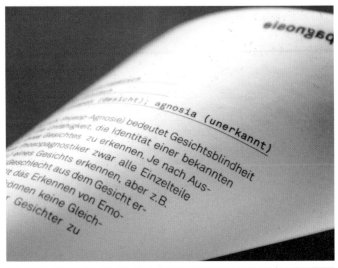

(Gesicht); agnosia (unerkannt)

...prosop-Agnosie) bedeutet Gesichtsblindheit
...fähigkeit, die Identität einer bekannten
...Gesichtes zu erkennen. Je nach Aus-
...eines Gesichts erkennen zwar alle Einzelteile
...Geschlecht aus dem Gesicht erkennen, aber z.B.
...t das Erkennen von Emo-
...können keine von Gleich-
...r Gesichter zu

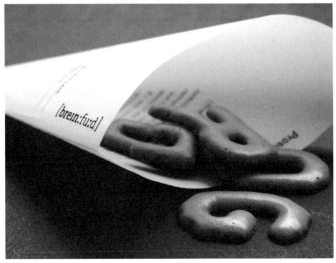

[brɛɪnˈfuːd]

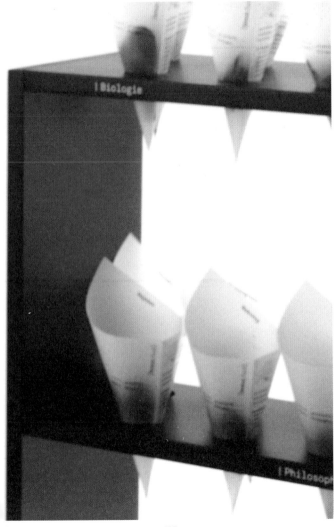

438

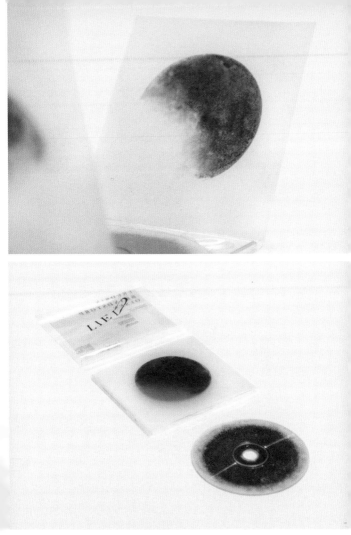

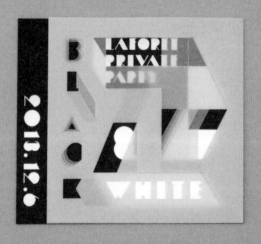

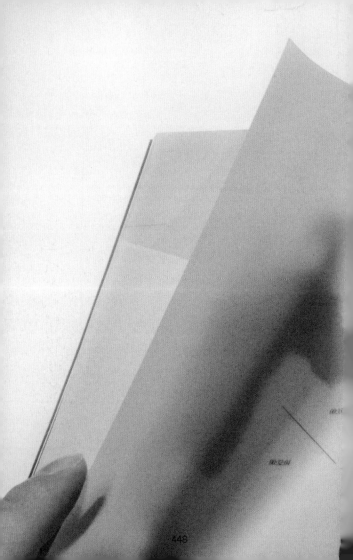

Yvonne Raine

Readings in Contemporary Cinema 197

& abstra Film

Performance at Dia:Beacon

EAI Archive

Ian Wilson

The Pure

awareness of

the Absolute/

scussions

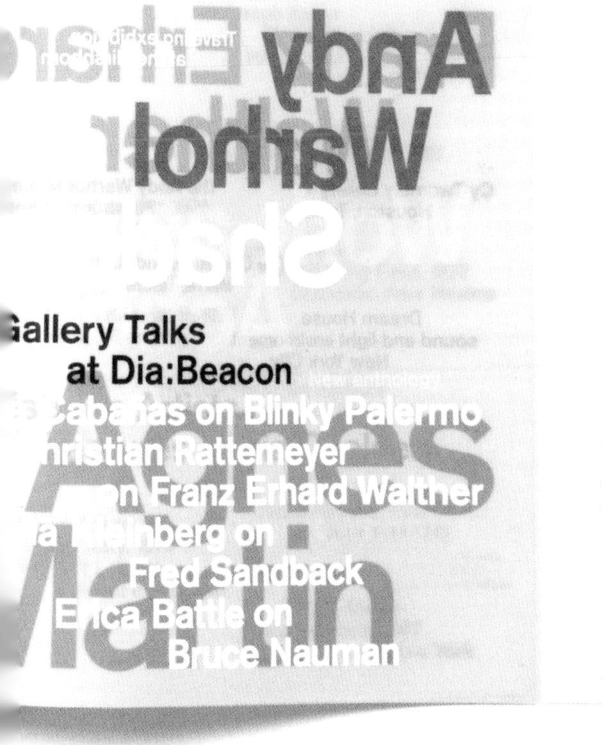

Andy
Warhol
Shadows

Gallery Talks
at Dia:Beacon
cabañas on Blinky Palermo
ristian Rattemeyer
n Franz Erhard Walther
a Kleinberg on
Fred Sandback
Erica Battle on
Bruce Nauman

Andy Warhol

Traveling exhibition at the Hirshhorn

Performance at Dia:Beacon

Shadow

Gallery Talks
at Dia:Beacon
a Cabañas on Blinky Palermo
Christian Rattemeyer
on Franz Erhard Walther
na Kleinberg on
Fred Sandback
Erica Battle on
Bruce Nauman

Franz Erhard Walther

Walther

Work as Action

Action

New anthology

Agnes
Martin

anz Walt

Work

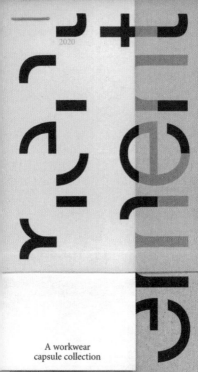

2020

A workwear
capsule collection

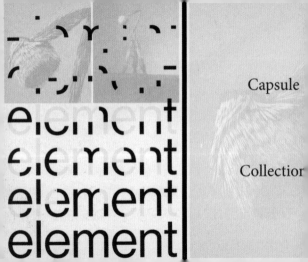

element
element
element
element

Capsule

Collection

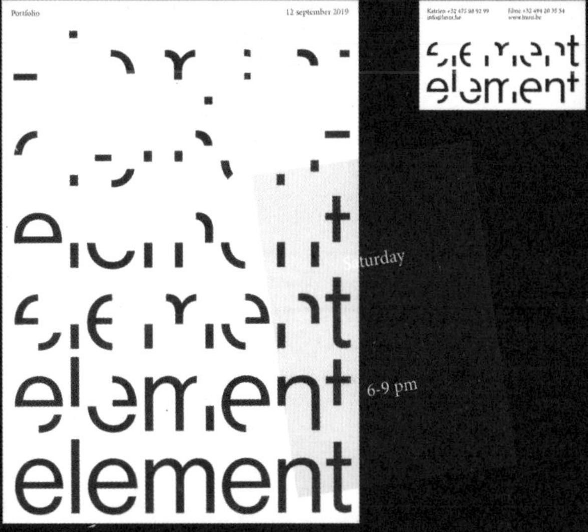

element
element
element
element
element
element

Saturday

6-9 pm

Katrien +32 473 38 92 99
info@bient.be

Elisa +32 494 38 35 54
www.bient.be

element
element

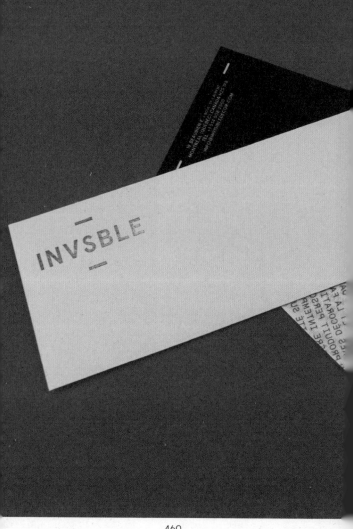

CONCEPTION
DESIGN
FABRICATION

CONCEPTION
DESIGN
FABRICATION

MEUBLES
ACCESSOIRES
PLEXIGLAS
SUR MESURE
FAIT MAIN

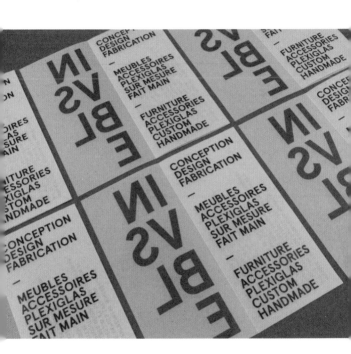

上海市想
上海城梦

2013
ОКТЯБРЬ
AUTUMN

Shanghai is the largest city by population in the China. The vast majority of Shanghai's 6,340.5 km2 (2,448.0 sq mi) land area is flat, apart from a few hills in the south-west corner. Shanghai's infrastructural and capital development, its importance in the fiscal well-being of the central government and revival of economic liberalizations began in 1990. Shanghai was finally permitted to initiate economic reforms in 1991, starting the massive development still seen today and the birth of Lujiazui in Pudong.

L

上海市
城梦想
海市

2013
ОКТЯБРЬ
AUTUMN

Shanghai is the largest city by population in the China. The vast majority of Shanghai's 6,340.5 km2 (2,448.1 sq mi) land area is flat, apart from a few hills in the southwest corner. Shanghai's infrastructural and capital development. Its importance to the fiscal well-being of the central government also played a important role. Shanghai's location in economic liberalisation began in 1990, starting the tremendous development with seen today and the birth of Lujiazui in Pudong.

L

上海 海市
城 梦 想

2013
ОКТЯБРЬ
AUTUMN

Shanghai is the largest city by population in the China. The vast majority of Shanghai's 6,341 km2 (2,448.1 sq mi) land area is flat, apart from a few hills in the southwest corner. Shanghai's administrative and capital development, its importance to the fiscal well-being of the central government also denied economic liberalizations begun in 1978. Shanghai was finally permitted to initiate economic reforms in 1991, starting the massive development still seen today and the birth of Lujiazui in Pudong.

WWW.BEHANCE.NET//ZARATATA///

473

06 07

08

07

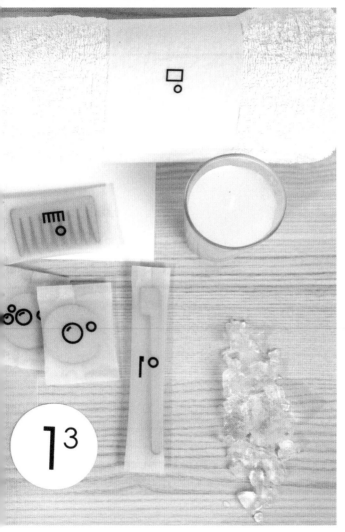

WE ARE
NOW
LONELIER
THAN
EVER
BEFORE

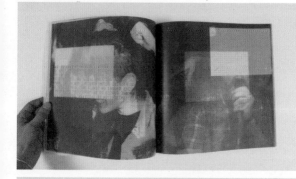

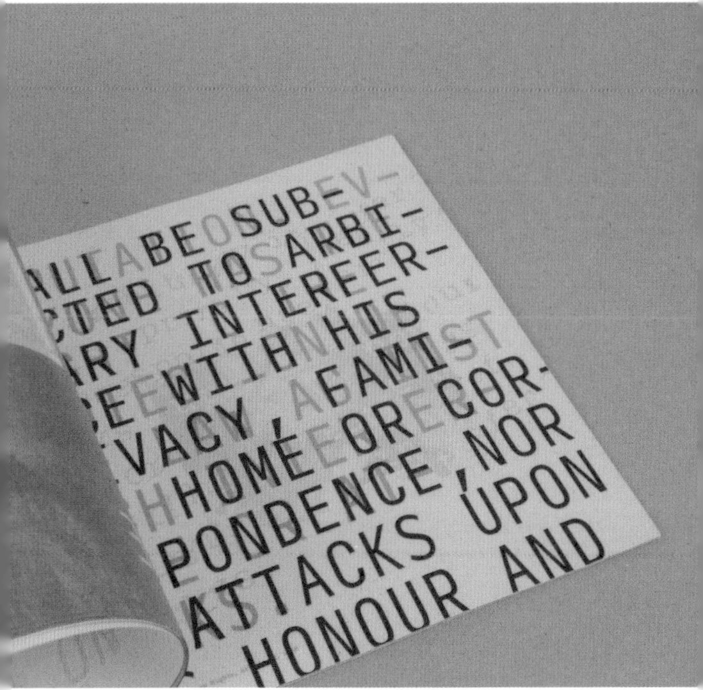

ALL ABE OSUBEV-
CTED TO SARBI-
ARY INTEREER-
EE WITH HIS
VACY, A FAMI
HOME OR COR-
PONDENCE, NOR
ATTACKS UPON
HONOUR AND

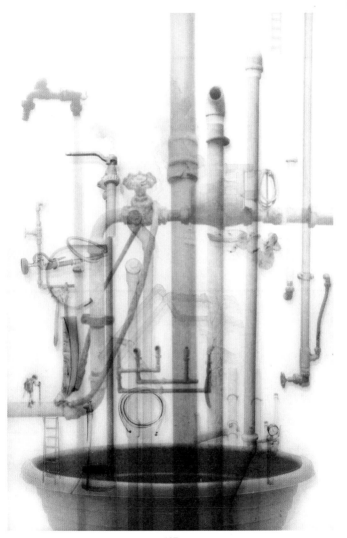

487

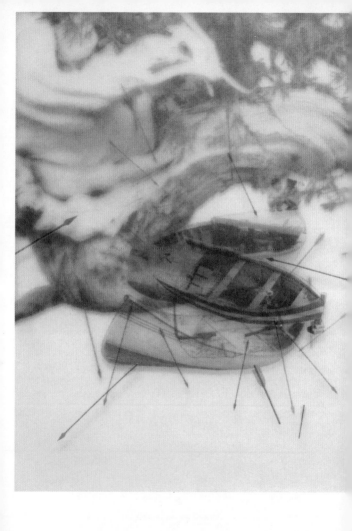

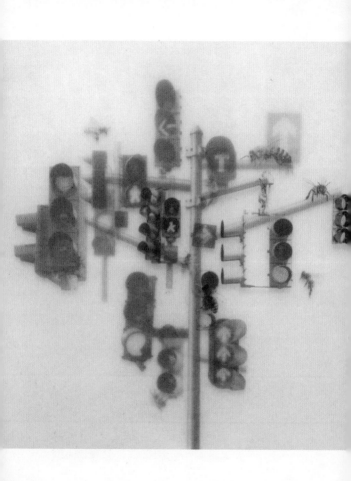

491

"Visual language has to be as simple as possible. That's the best way towards transparency."

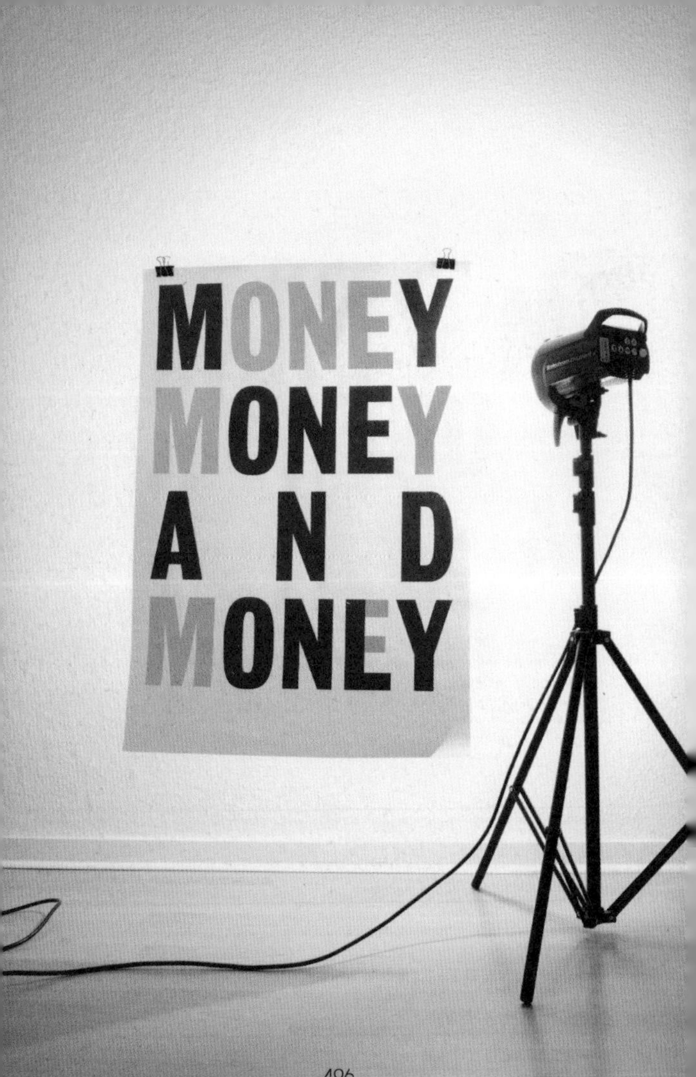
MONEY
MONEY
AND
MONEY

Tonelli design

mirage 2014

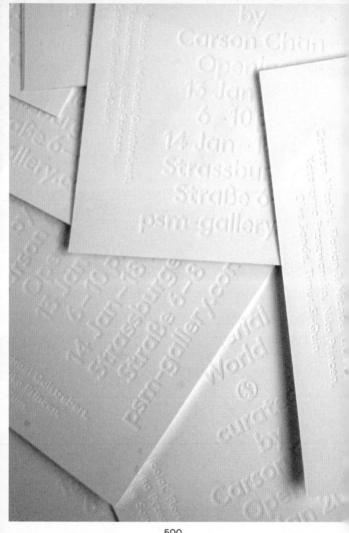

THE
WEDDING
OF

THOMAS
JOHNSON

EDWINA
FLEMING

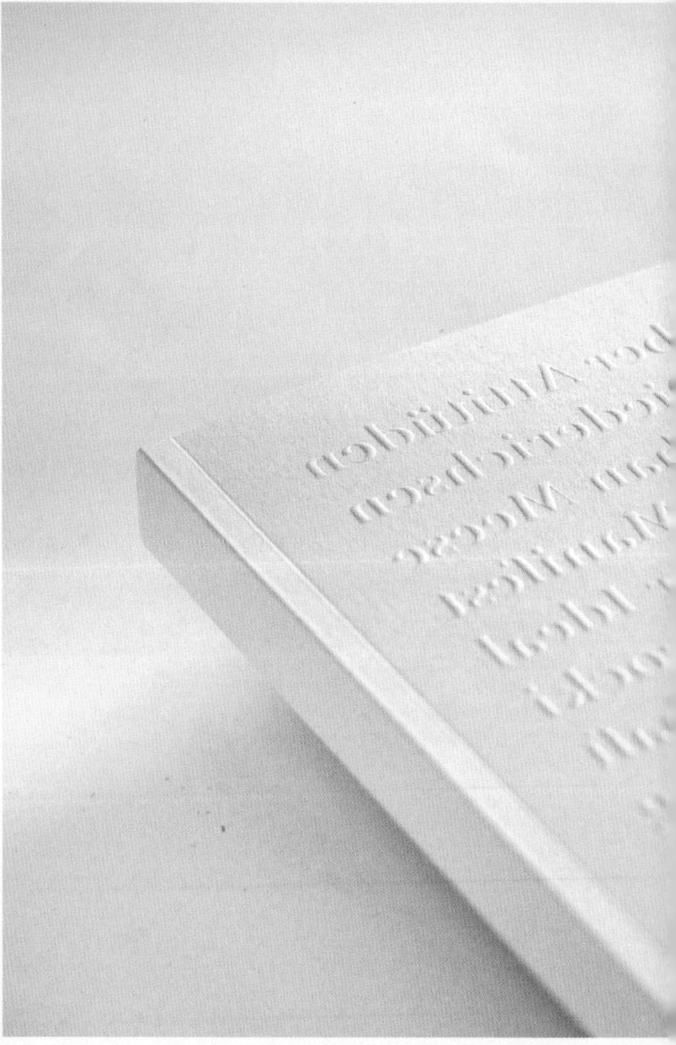

TEXT

GESPRÄCHE

TEXT

GESPRÄCHE

Andreas van Dühren

511

noble
development
public
company
limited

annual report
2012

19th fl. floor of tower
900 nor..char.. thanon wan
bangkok 10330 thailand

t: 662 251 9955
f: 662 251 9992

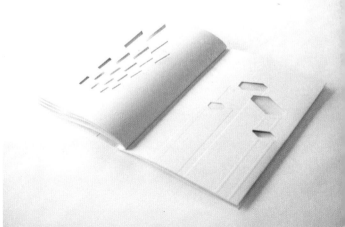

flávia nalon
rua carla 10 itaim bibi
04531.070 são paulo sp
t n 3079 3785   f n 3079 5894
flavianalon@ps2.com.br
www.ps2.com.br

ps.N | arquitetura + design

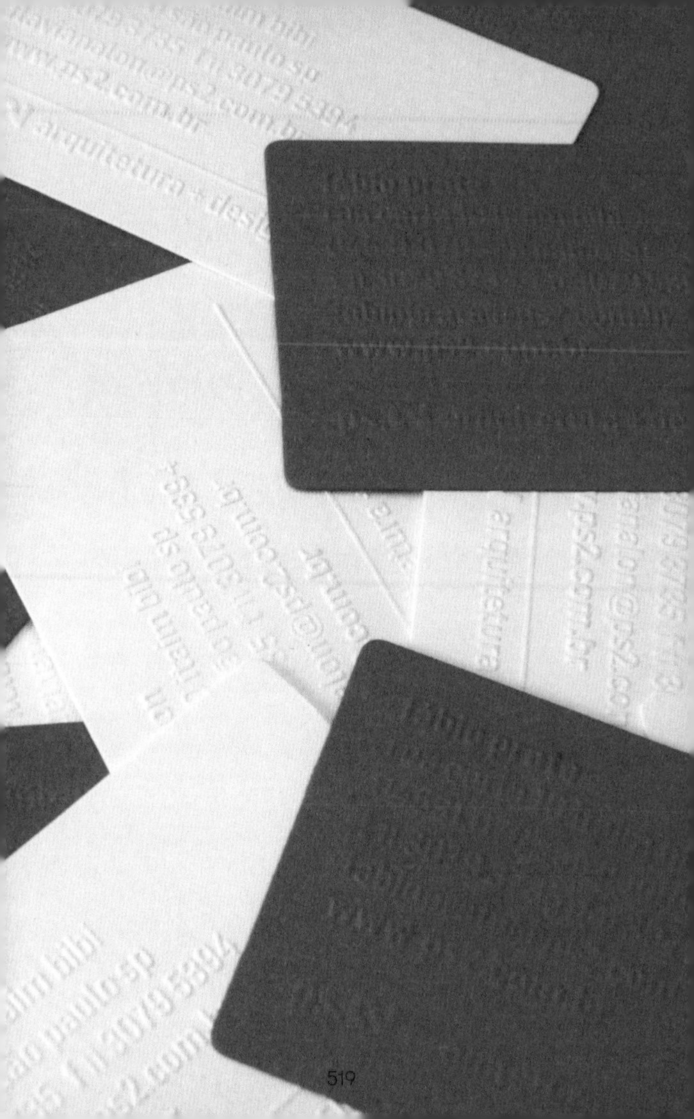

Panasonic Design Kyoto

Large
Conference
Room

Conference
Room

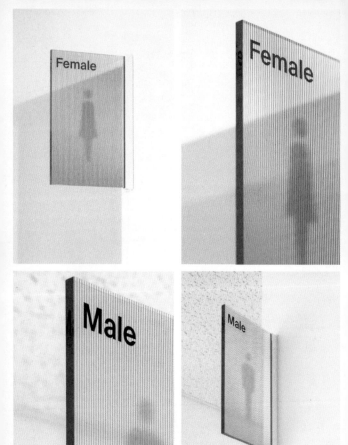

Male

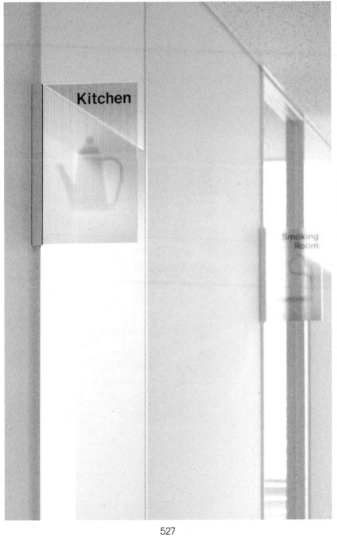

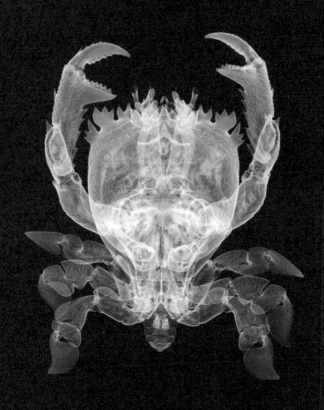

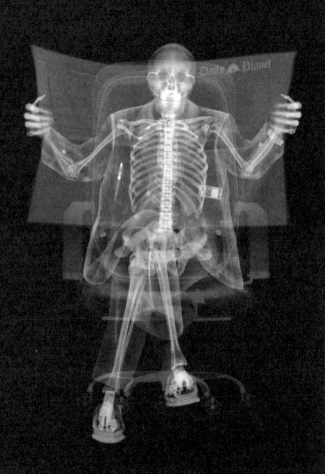

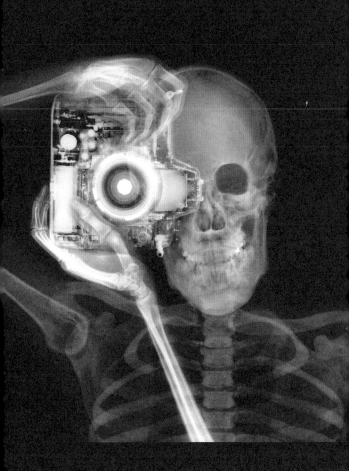

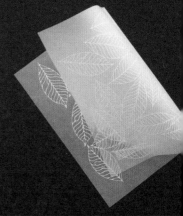

THE "PAPER LEAF" MADE WITH PAPER.
THIS PLANT USED TO BE A SLICE OF PAPER AND,
BY LIFTING IT UP BY FINGERS,
THE LEAF BECOMES THREE-DIMENSIONAL
AND STANDS UP.

PAPER
LEAF
EXHIBITION

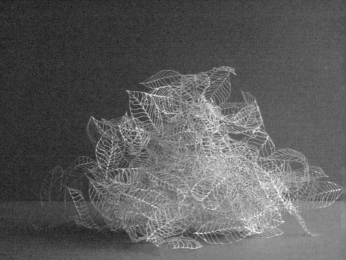

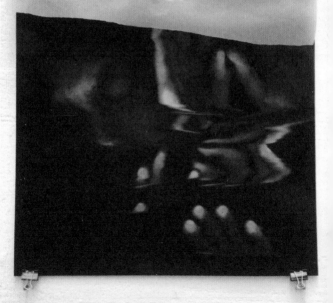

547

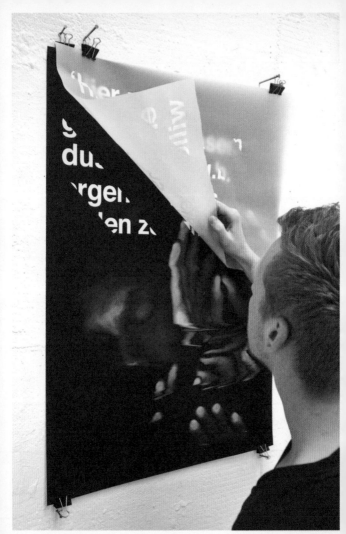

549

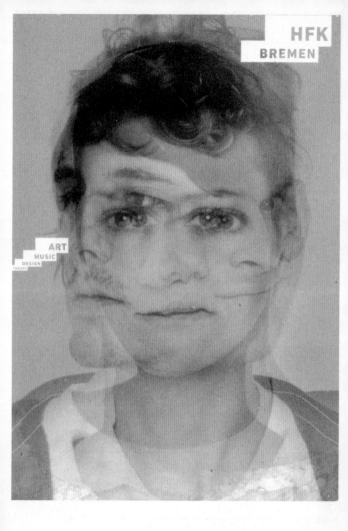

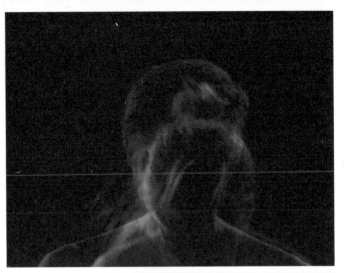

SA.11.2. + SO.12.2.
HOCHSCHULTAGE 2012
IM SPEICHER XI

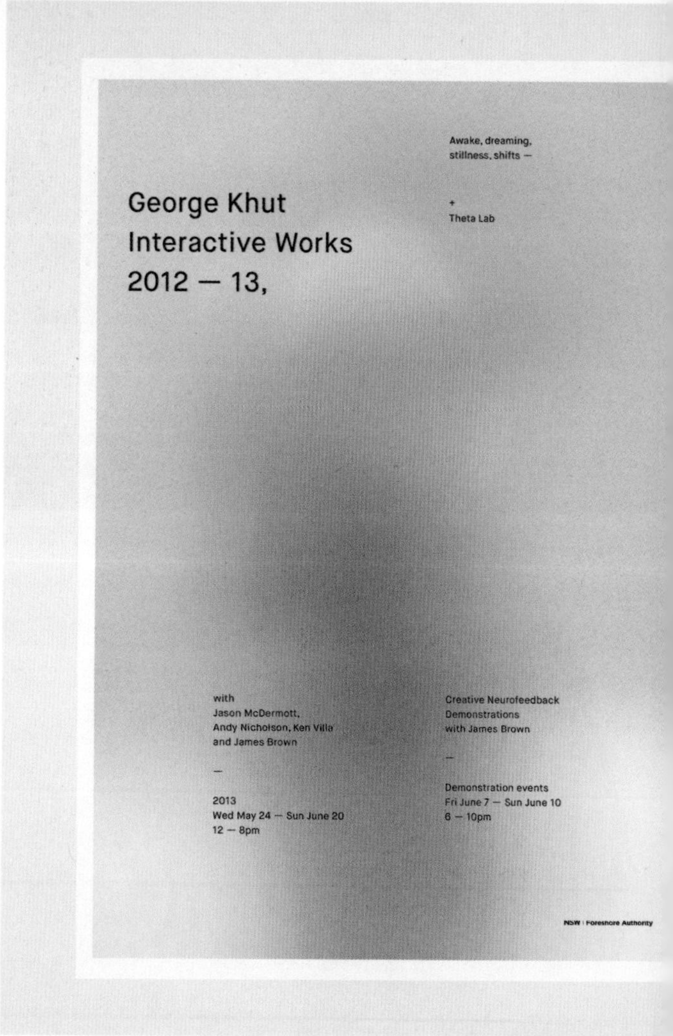

Awake, dreaming,
stillness, shifts —

George Khut
Interactive Works
2012 — 13,

+
Theta Lab

with
Jason McDermott,
Andy Nicholson, Ken Villa
and James Brown

—

2013
Wed May 24 — Sun June 20
12 — 8pm

Creative Neurofeedback
Demonstrations
with James Brown

—

Demonstration events
Fri June 7 — Sun June 10
6 — 10pm

NSW : Foreshore Authority

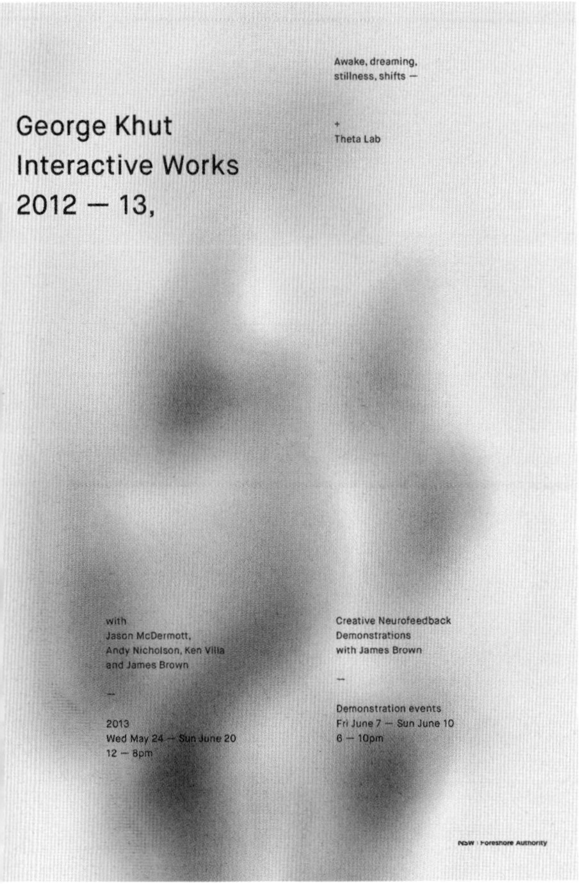

Awake, dreaming,
stillness, shifts —

+
Theta Lab

George Khut
Interactive Works
2012 — 13,

with
Jason McDermott,
Andy Nicholson, Ken Villa
and James Brown

—

2013
Wed May 24 — Sun June 20
12 — 8pm

Creative Neurofeedback
Demonstrations
with James Brown

—

Demonstration events
Fri June 7 — Sun June 10
6 — 10pm

NSW : Foreshore Authority

George Khut
Interactive Works
2012 — 13.

George Khut
Interactive Works
2012 — 13.

with
Jason McDermott,
Andy Nicholson, Ken Villa
and James Brown

2013
Wed May 24 — Sun June 20
12 — 8pm

Awake, dreaming,
— stillness, shifts

+
Theta Lab

George Khut
interactive Works
2012 — 13,

1

BrightHearts "Embers"
Prototype iPad application / 2013

2

Pipelines
Sound sculptures / 2013

3

Cardiomorphologies
Heart-rate controlled projections / 2005 – 2012

4

Distillery video portraits
Interaction documentation / 2012

5

Theta Lab #1
Brainwave controlled multimedia
and experiential documentation / 2013

Creative Neurofeedback
Demonstrations
with James Brown

--

Demonstration events
Fri June 7 – Sun June 10
6 – 10pm

with
Jason McDermott,
Andy Nicholson, Ken Villa
and James Brown

--

2013
Wed May 24 – Sun June 20
12 – 8pm

Exhibition identity & design
Holiday — Elise Santangelo & Stuart Geddes

georgekhut.com

"Transparency is a powerful tool to communicate in photography."

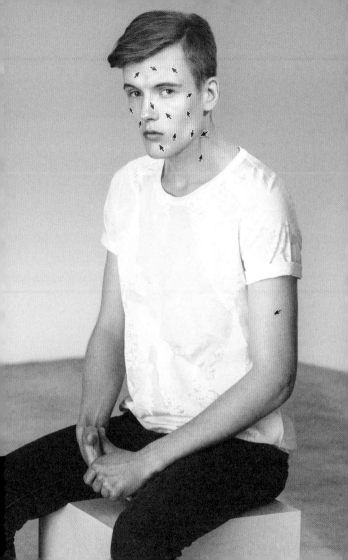

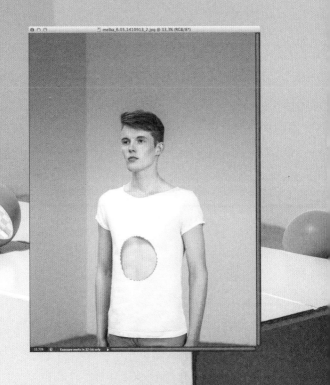

TRANSPARENT
DISTORTED

GLASS IS NOT JUST A MATERIAL,
BUT A SUMMARY OF THE WORLD WE LIVE IN.
I HAVE EXPLORED THE PROPERTIES OF THE
GLASS AND CONDUCTED EXPERIMENTS ON ITS
MATERIALITY THROUGH THIS PROCESS, I HAVE
MADE IMAGES AND GRAPHICS AS A RESULT.
FURTHERMORE, I HAVE EXPANDED THIS
PROJECT BY COLLECTING STORIES OF PEOPLE
CONSTANTLY MAKING AND UNMAKING THEIR
BOUNDARIES, WHICH ARE SIMILAR TO THE
MATERIALITY OF THE GLASS.

THIS PROJECT SUGGESTS THE AUDIENCE TO
RECONSIDER THE PRESENCE OF THE GLASS
AND I WISH TO SHARE MY DELIGHTFUL
EXPERIENCES WITH THE OTHERS.

BYODHYEON CHO

568

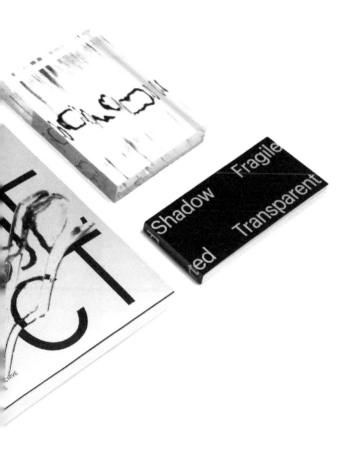

TRANSPA
RENT

TRANSPARENT
THE PROPERTIES OF GLASS THROUGH WHICH LIGHT PASSES:
(A)WITH SCANNER, GLASS
(B)WITH SCANNER, GLASS, PRINTED PATTERN

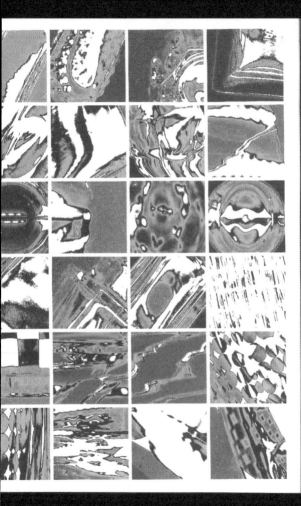

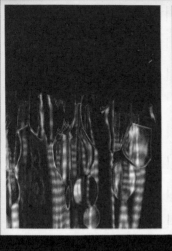

38

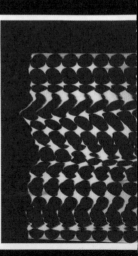

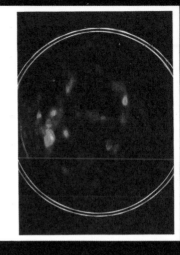

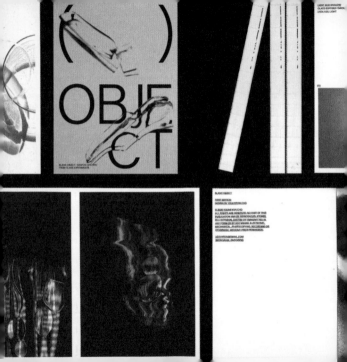

Through A. Glass Darkly
UIC School of Design 2017–18
Public Seminar Series
ANDREW BLAUVELT
Thursday, February 1, 6:00PM
Free and Open to the Public

Room 1100
UIC School of Design
College of Architecture,
Design, and the Arts
845 West Harrison Street
Chicago

THROUGH A GLASS DARKLY

Through A Glass Darkly
UIC School of Design 2017-18
Public Seminar Series
MARK OWENS
Friday, October 27, 6:00PM
Free and Open to the Public

Room 1100
UIC School of Design
College of Architecture,
Design, and the Arts
845 West Harrison Street
Chicago

MARK OWENS

UIC SCHOOL OF DESIGN PUBLIC SEMINAR 2017-18

OCT 27

6:00PM

Through A Glass Darkly
UIC School of Design
2017–18 Public Seminar Series
TILL WITTWER
Thursday, November 9, 6:00PM
Free and Open to the Public

Room 1100
UIC School of Design
College of Architecture,
Design, and the Arts
845 West Harrison Street
Chicago

591

INDEX

BIOGRAPHY

&Larry

andlarry.com

Founded in 2005, &Larry is a design company based in Singapore whose practice is deeply rooted in creating empathic connections between people. It believes that design innovation should always serve human interest – holding a high regard for the intuitive use of data, research, and technology in support of creativity instead of being limited by it.

PP. 384-387

26 Lettres

Founded as a collaborative practice comprising a broader circle of specialists and creative minds to create effective design solutions, 26 Lettres was a Montreal-based multidisciplinary creative office. Its philosophy was rooted in human connections, in building unique, sensitive, and innovative solutions.

PP. 460-465

Aaron Nieh Workshop

aaronnieh.com

Although Aaron Nieh deals with details in subtle ways, his visual style is highly provocative and imaginative, as he builds new landscapes in the sinophone pop music, publishing, and performing arts worlds. A member of AGI since 2012, he continues to craft new perspectives through his mastery of imagery, symbols, and materials.

PP. 092-097, 254-255

ADESTRA / All Design Transparent

adestradesign.com

A Saint Petersburg-based multidisciplinary design studio specialising in branding, art direction and user experiences, ADESTRA was founded by Anastasia Yakovleva, who works closely with printing houses to produce complex work across different media.

PP. 508-511

aether3 Studio

aether3creative.com

Founded in 2020, Aether Appear is a multidisciplinary visual studio in Taiwan with a team comprising experienced creatives from various design backgrounds. It works on commercial and cultural projects across the globe, spanning art direction, graphics, branding, typography and web design.

PP. 082-085

Aki Inomata

aki-inomata.com

Born in 1983 in Tokyo, Aki graduated with an MFA in Inter Media Art from Tokyo University of the Arts in 2008. Her work has been exhibited around the world.

PP. 212-217

AMKK

azumamakoto.com

Azuma Makoto is a floral artist and botanical sculptor who focuses on elevating the value of plants by highlighting their unique and mysterious sides.

PP. 314-319

Anagrama

anagrama.com

Anagrama is an international branding firm specialising in the design of brands, objects, spaces, software, and multi-media. It thrives on breaking the traditional creative agency scheme by integrating multidisciplinary teams of creative and business experts.

PP. 244-245

Andren

cargocollective.com/andren

Andren was a studio founded by Andrea Novali to represent the dark side of typography.

PP. 480-481

Anna Maggi, Elahe Rajabiani, Prasad Bhadke

Anna Maggi, Elahe Rajabiani and Prasad Bhadke worked together on 'Frozen Past', the project in this book, when they were attending the same product service system design masters course in 2012.

PP. 174-177

Anna Szendrei
be.net/szendreianna

Anna is a Hungarian graphic designer whose work often deals with social and political issues, as she balances experiments with various styles/techniques and a 'strict, geometric world'.

PP. 324-327

---

artless Inc.
artless.co.jp

Established in 2000 by Shun Kawakami, artless Inc. is a global branding agency that conducts design with architecture. Working across a variety of touchpoints, the Tokyo-based studio has won several awards from prestigious design organisations along the way, including Cannes and D&AD.

PP. 098-101, 474-477

Backbone Branding Studio

backbonebranding.com

Backbone Branding is an independent branding studio in Armenia and a creative business partner to clients who are ready for extraordinary solutions. The team digs deep into a brand's essence and values – moving beyond design for design's sake to offer consumers solutions that are relevant and incredibly engaging.

PP. 056-059

Baillat Studio

baillat.ca

Baillat is a multiplatform production and design studio based in Montreal that distinguishes itself with an audacious and refined multidisciplinary approach. Closely aligned with the cultural milieus of music and digital art, the studio excels within experimental and conventional paradigms.

PP. 118-125

BULLET INC.

bullet-inc.jp

BULLET Inc. was founded by Osaka-born award-winning designer Aya Codama in 2013. Armed with a major in graphic design from Tokyo Zokei University Department of Design (where she currently also teaches), she specialises in packaging and features various printing techniques in her work.

PP. 402-407

c plus c workshop

FB: @cpluscworkshop

c plus c workshop is a Hong Kong based studio that focuses on graphic design, advertising, branding, corporate communications, and visual identities. In line with the philosophies behind its name (creativity and communication), the team seeks to cultivate sensitivity rather than just produce visually impressive work.

PP. 048-053

Camilo Rojas

cr-eate.com

A graphic designer and art director based in Miami, Camilo works with agencies, design studios, and startups on projects across a wide range of disciplines using a collaborative, idea-driven process that strives for simplicity, playfulness, and craftsmanship.

PP. 260-263

CCRZ

ccrz.ch

Working from offices in Switzerland and Italy, CCRZ comprises a team of designers, architects, and communication specialists that crafts and evolves meaningful brands through effective ideas and strategic thinking. It is committed to meaningful visual communication that will endure, avoiding the trivial by combining creative ingenuity with serious thinking.

PP. 370-373

Cleber Rafael de Campos

cleberdecampos.com

Cleber is an award-winning Brazilian-born, London-based graphic designer with experience in the areas of editorial design, branding, typography and advertising art direction; where his career began. He holds an MA in Graphic Design from University of the Arts London (LCC).

PP. 482-485

CoDesign Ltd

codesign.co.hk

CoDesign Ltd was co-founded by Eddy Yu and Hung Lam in 2003, specialising in providing holistic branding solutions. In 2011, they formed CoLAB, a collaborative platform for social innovation through design. CoLAB aims to synergise commercial, cultural, and social entities to consciously promote social betterment through creativity.

PP. 396-401

Daan Rietbergen

daanrietbergen.com

A visual designer from Utrecht, Daan specialises in visual identities, poster design, and typography.

PP. 546-549

Dev Valladares

valladares.dev

Dev Valladares is an interdisciplinary designer and visual artist from Mumbai, India, currently designing at COLLINS, NY.

PP. 378-383

DUNGER DESIGN

Founded in 2013 by Marcel Dunger and Florian Meier, DUNGER DESIGN's creative services ranged from product and furniture design to interior and exterior design. In 2014, the duo founded the label Manufract based on the philosophy of self-healing trees, combining hardwood and organic resin in the form of decorative elements.

PP. 310-311

Econosys Design Inc.

econsys.jp

Econosys Design truly believes that clients can achieve their full potential through effective design. Based on the underlying principle that communication is the key to better understanding one's purpose and vision, the team strives to highlight the best of brands by building strong relationships with people.

PP. 520-527

Edith Rose Studio
edithrose.com.au

Edith Rose Studio was born out of the desire to bring a high fashion aesthetic to the world of wedding and event stationery. Their work focuses on the development of distinctive, thoughtful design solutions that capture the individual personalities of each client. Skilfully handcrafted, all pieces are created using traditional letterpress and hot foil printing techniques.

PP. 502-503

emuni
emuni.co.jp

Founded in 2012 by Takashi Murakami and Masashi Murakami, emuni Inc. is an award-winning art direction and design practice based in Tokyo. Its works span across multiple mediums and platforms, including packaging, wayfinding, and editorial design.

PP. 104-109

Ermolaev Bureau
ermolaevbureau.com

Ermolaev Bureau is an award-winning Moscow-based graphic design studio specialising in the creation of visual brand strategy, brand positioning, and project implementation in the fields of corporate and consumer identities. Its founder and creative director Vlad Ermolaev has been working in communication design since 1995.

PP. 376-377

Eyla Llarena Aliaño

eylallarena.com

Eyla Llarena Aliaño is a freelance graphic designer experienced in branding, digital media, and 3D. She strives to help people, companies, and institutions create or enhance their brand, image, or products.

PP. 246-249

FARMGROUP

farmgroup.co.th

FARMGROUP is a Bangkok–based creative and design consultancy working across various disciplines of art and design, including branding, art direction, print, wayfinding, exhibitions, and installations.

PP. 512-515

Flank Pty Ltd

A creative initiative based out of Melbourne and San Diego, Flank Pty Ltd worked to create a balance between environmental responsibility and convenience in life.

PP. 152-155

Form

Form was the Southern California-based graphic design studio of Brian Biles focusing on print design, custom typography, and art direction for clients in the fashion, music, and entertainment industries. His works have been published and exhibited internationally.

PP. 280-283

Futura

byfutura.com

Since 2008, Futura has become an internationally renowned creative studio characterised by its disruptive approach to design, pushing boundaries and taking risks every step of the way. Specialising in branding, art direction, and photography, the studio's vision consistently blurs the lines between different disciplines, paving the way to new forms of creativity.

PP. 040-047

Ghazaal Vojdani

studio.ghazaalvojdani.com

Studio Ghazaal Vojdani is a design and art direction practice, creating close and ongoing work relationships with cultural and educational institutions, independent galleries, editors, curators, designers, and artists internationally.

PP. 184-187

Gilli Kuchik & Ran Amitai

www.kuchikamitai.com/

Established in 2009 by Ran Amitai and Gilli Kuchik while studying industrial design at the Bezalel Academy of Art and Design, Bakery Studio found new ways of interpreting traditional production methods and object typologies based on hands-on experimentation with materials and technologies. The designers currently live and work in Tel Aviv.

PP. 264-265

Greg Klassen

gregklassen.com

An independent artisan, Greg's pieces are crafted with a great respect for nature, as he takes inspiration in the trees, rivers, and fields from the Pacific Northwest, where he lives with his family.

PP. 312-313

HAFT DESIGN

haft-design.com

Daisuke Akiyama is a product designer based in Tokyo, who looks to create better interactions between objects and humans. Using a comprehensive approach to design, he works on product development, material application, manufacturing, and chemical technology.

PP. 170-173

Halina Mrożek

notjustalabel.com/halina-mrozek

Halina Mrożek originates from the mountains of Southern Poland. An innovative and progressive artist, painter, sculptor, and costume creator, she graduated from the Faculty of Sculpture at the Academy of Fine Arts, Krakow. Her work is known to overwhelm, inspire, and at times, tease her audiences.

PP. 066-069

Hey

heystudio.es

Hey is a creative studio in Barcelona that creates fresh brands, conceptual communication campaigns, unique illustrations, and other creative outcomes by building strong relationships and taking care of every aspect of the design process. It believes in the power of visuals for changing things and achieving goals.

PP. 250-253

Holiday

Kristoffer Wilson graduated from Duncan of Jordanstone College of Art & Design in Dundee in 2011. He is a member of the International Society of Typographic Designers and is currently working in Glasgow, Scotland.

PP. 552-555

HOUTH

houth.tw

HOUTH is a creative studio based in Taipei that flexibly integrates ideas, creativity, strategy, design, and resources to create fresh solutions and stories for clients.

PP. 086-091

Jack Curtis, Colin Young, Brendan Ratzlaff

Jack, Colin and Brendan are graphic designers from Vancouver who worked together for the project in this book.

PP. 150-151

Jackson&Harris

rodneyharris.co.uk

Award-winning artists Rodney Harris MRSS and Valda Jackson MRSS (Member of the Royal Society of Sculptors) collaborate on public art projects as Jackson&Harris. They have been commissioned by a range of public and private clients for brick relief sculpture within new architecture, such as the Peabody Trust at the St. John Hill's Estate in Clapham, London.

PP. 606-611

Jelle Kok

jellekok.nl

A multidisciplinary designer living and working in the Netherlands with a love for typography, detail, and inventiveness, Jelle has a conceptual, systematic and playful approach to design. He strives to communicate meaningful ideas, beliefs and stories to audiences through traditional and new media.

PP. 374-375

Jiani Lu

lujiani.com

An award-winning multidisciplinary graphic designer, Jiani's passion lies in print, branding, and information design. From a young age, she developed a keen interest in paper art and hands-on craft, which have been translated into her designs over the years.

PP. 418-423

Joanie Brisebois

joaniebrisebois.com

Joanie is a multidisciplinary designer and art director in Montreal who creates for change and takes a meaningful stand by instilling awareness through her work. She also co-founded Echelles, an editorial collective born out of the desire to create an accessible platform for all.

PP. 102-103

JOEFANGSTUDIO

joefangstudio.com

Named after its creative director Joe Fang, JOEFANGSTUDIO designs for the music industry, events, brands, art installations, and more. It aims to condense the creativity found in daily life into unique, fun designs.

PP. 010-017, 126-135

Josep Puy

joseppuy.com

Josep is a Barcelona-based graphic designer specialising in editorials, graphic design, and branding.

PP. 470-473

Kamimura & Co. (formerly credited as Kamimura Typografie Gestalten)

kkco.jp

Kamimura & Co. is a multidisciplinary design studio in Japan that was established to contribute to the progress of brands, supporting them comprehensively and continuously via professional visualisation.

PP. 192-195

Kristina Razueva

be.net/Taratata

Kristina is a graphic designer skilled in branding and identities, food packaging, graphic design, and art direction.

PP. 466-469

Kristofer Gullard Lindgren

be.net/KristoferLindgren

Kristofer studied visual communication at Beckmans College of Design in Stockholm.

PP. 054-055

Ksana Design Studio

ksanadesign.com

Founded in 2011, Ksana Design Studio in Hong Kong is convinced that good design can improve not only the future, but also living standards. Offering branding, graphic design, and multimedia design services, the team emphasises mutual trust-building with clients throughout the design process.

PP. 446-449

Kwok-hin Tang

tangkwokhin.com

Kwok-hin Tang is an internationally exhibited Hong Kong mixed media artist, working as an independent curator and writer. He was born in 1983 and received his MFA and BA from the Chinese University of Hong Kong.

PP. 486-493

Leanne Bentley, Ed Rivers, Stephanie Bickford-Smith, Clara Goodger, Andy Dawes, Benji Roebuck

Leanne, Ed, Stephanie, Clara, Andy and Benji are Kingston University graduates who worked together on the project in this book.

PP. 060-065

Leonardo Sonnoli, Irene Bacchi (Tassinari/Vetta)

Born in Trieste in 1962, Leonardo's design practice ranges from visual identities and communication design to book design, signal systems and exhibition displays. An AGI member since 2000, he was the President of its Italian Chapter in 2003. He also lectures at the Faculty of Design and Arts of the IUAV University of Venice and the ISIA in Urbino.

PP. 498-499

Lorenz Potthast, Filippo Baraccani, Mikko Gaertner

Lorenz, Filippo and Mikko were studying integrated design when they worked together on the project in this book.

PP. 550-551

Luna Ikuta
lunaikuta.com

Luna Ikuta is a multidisciplinary artist based in Los Angeles. Her notable work blends sculpture, digital media, chemistry, and biology to create transformed natural worlds of plants, made transparent using a special process that reveals their intricate structures. Her works are a window in the liminal space between life and death - a lively botanical graveyard.

PP. 408-417

Manual
manualcreative.com

Manual is a San Francisco-based design and brand consultancy creating meaningful impact through the thoughtful application of brand narratives, graphic design, art direction, and material craft. It partners with visionary clients to translate bold ideas into beautifully articulated identities and experiences, creating value through recognition and desirability.

PP. 290-293

Maria Svarbova

mariasvarbova.com

Born in 1988, Maria Svarbova currently lives in Slovakia. Despite studying restoration and archeology, her preferred artistic medium is photography. From 2010 to the present, the immediacy of her photographic instinct continues to garner international acclaim and is setting new precedents In photographic expression.

PP. 556-559

Matteo Morelli, Yurika Omoto

In addition to Matteo and Yurika, Tomomi Kuniki, Chinae Takedomi, Asuka Miyakoshi and Sayoko Aoki were students when they all worked together on the project for this book.

PP. 356-361

mistroom

be.net/mistroomart

Co-founded by Peng Yu-jui and Huang Jui-i in 2010, mistroom is a design studio that stays sensitive to a distinct design aesthetic. Its design philosophy reveals the true essence of daily life and elegantly evokes its viewers' senses and memories.

PP. 336-339, 362-367

MMVARQUITECTO

mmvarquitecto.com

A Lisbon-based architectural firm founded by Miguel Marques Venâncio in 2008, MMVARQUITECTO seeks to capture the specific energy of each site, creating atmospheres that potentiate the strength of the location with geometric rigour, abstract composition, and constructive depuration, magnifying the refinement of a sculptural architecture that pursues an awakening of positive emotions and of timeless values.

PP. 588-591

Morphoria Design Collective

morphoria.com

As a collective, Morphoria combines dynamism and variety with a stable and reliable core. Constantly growing, the team benefits strongly from the sharing of knowledge and diverse skill sets. It keeps the passion alive through collaborations and explorations into other non-graphic design areas.

PP. 434-437

mousegraphics

mousegraphics.eu

mousegraphics is a creative office that believes that design is an endless exercise in communication. Since 1984, its consistent approach has been rewarded with a significant circle of long-standing collaborations, along with new successful professional relationships in a variety of applications within the design field.

PP. 328-335

Mucho

wearemucho.com

From its offices in Barcelona, Paris, San Francisco, New York, and Sydney, Mucho's work spans various disciplines to include art direction, strategic identity design, editorial design, packaging design, graphic communications, digital design, and motion graphics.

PP. 028-035

Naonori Yago

naonoriyago.com

Born in Shizuoka, Naonori Yago is an art director and graphic design who has won awards from the Tokyo and New York ADCs, D&AD, Cannes Lions, and the One Show. She graduated from the Department of Visual Communication Design, Musashino Art University in 2009.

PP. 112-117, 342-345, 442-445, 536-545

nendo

nendo.jp

Founded by architect Oki Sato in 2002, nendo in Tokyo sets out to bring small surprises to people through multidisciplinary practices of different media including architecture, interiors, furniture, industrial products, and graphic design.

PP. 136-141, 156-157, 266-275, 302-305, 602-605

Nicelab Studio

nicelab-studio.com

Nicelab is a design studio based in Beijing. Its experienced team specialises in popular visual styles, tightening the bonds between users and products through design to grow brand value and strengthen customer stickiness.

PP. 320-323

Nicholas Kulseth, Eirik Ruiner Torgersen, Anna Ducros

Nicholas, Eirik and Anna were studying graphic design at Westerdals Oslo School of Arts, Communication & Technology (ACT) when they worked together on the project in this book.

PP. 438-441

Nick Veasey

nickveasey.com

A man with x-ray vision, Nick Veasey creates art that shows what it is really like inside. Nick's work with radiographic imaging equipment takes the x-ray to another level.

PP. 528-535

Noeeko

noeeko.com

Founded by art and creative director Michal Sycz, Noeeko works across digital, print, branding, and interactive media. The multidisciplinary design studio aims to create coherent, original, and distinctive design solutions that communicate its clients' key messages.

PP. 076-081

NOSIGNER

nosigner.com

NOSIGNER is a social design activist that drives change towards a more hopeful future. Using design as a tool to form meaningful relationships, the studio creates multidisciplinary strategies by seeking the highest quality within each design field, including architecture, product- and graphic design.

PP. 340-341, 584-587

Now Design + Direction

wearenow.at

Now Design + Direction creates holistic design solutions by asking the right questions and shaping relevant visual identities. Co-founded by creative director Paul Leichtfried, it focuses on brand identities, multichannel editorial and information design.

PP. 494-497

Numen / For Use

numen.eu

Numen / For Use is a collective working in the fields of conceptual art, scenography, industrial- and spatial design. The group first formed in 1998 as a collaborative effort between industrial designers Sven Jonke, Christoph Katzler and Nikola Radeljković.

PP. 206-211

---

oodesign

oodesign.com

By combining the symbol 'oo', which is used to refer to a wild-card in Japan, with 'design', Taku Omura's studio name expresses his creative approach to challenging boundaries through products and concepts that stretch and change the possibilities of everyday life.

PP. 024-027

Ortica Studio

be.net/anonymdeis25bf

Ortica Studio is a multidisciplinary independent design practice in Milan, led by Ivan D'Antuono and Alberto Consentino. It works on interiors, brand identities, editorials, and web design by tending to every aspect of the design process.

PP. 070-075

P-06 Atelier

p-06-atelier.pt

An award-winning international firm specialising in communication and environmental design for complex, large-scale wayfinding systems, museums and exhibitions, P-06 Atelier was founded in 2006 by partners Nuno Gusmão, Estela Estanislau, Pedro Anjos and Catarina Carreira.

PP. 188-191

Page Three Hundred

pagethreehundred.com

Page Three Hundred is a Turin-based independent clothing label and studio founded in 2014 by Gabriele Marchi and Maria Fernanda Barbero.

PP. 036-039

Paola Rojas H

be.net/paolar

Paola is a photographer from Bogotá who explores objects that catch her attention. Her work has been presented and published in Colombia, México, Spain, South Korea and China.

PP. 592-595

Paweł Fabjański
fabjanski.com

With a long list of international clients, brands, and prestigious magazines, Pawel's main focus is on the thin line that bridges art and commerce. His deep know-how of the production process, artistic skills, and photographic expertise are globally recognised by the creative industry and art lovers alike.

PP. 562-567

---

perezramerstorfer design & creative studio
perezramerstorfer.com

An Austro-Spanish multidisciplinary studio with a focus and passion for visual identities, perezramerstorfer design & creative studio helps brands, institutions, events, and companies on projects ranging from small initiatives to global campaigns. It believes in creating unique, consistent, and coherent work.

PP. 346-349

Phillip K Smith III
pks3.com

Born in 1972, Phillip is an artist who confronts the ideas of modernist design. He creates light-based work that draws upon the ideas of space, form, colour, light + shadow, environment, and change. Featured in hundreds of online and print publications, Phillip is known for creating large-scaled temporary installations.

PP. 612-614

PHOTOGRAPHER HAL

photographerhal.com

Born, educated, and currently residing in Tokyo, Haruhiko Kawaguchi found the camera as the key to break through shyness and language barriers. Building his photographic skills from various projects, people and love are crucial to the focus of his work.

PP. 178-183

Pinmo Design Studio

cargocollective.com/pinmodesign

Pinmo is a design studio based in Taipei that mostly works in brand identities, posters, illustrations and editorial design, as well as other printed matter. It seeks to project the origin of different products, brands or ideas through its work with passion and honesty.

PP. 160-165, 368-369

Polar, Ltda.

polar.ltda

Polar, Ltda. is a Brazilian office committed to delivering design solutions that balance impact and contextuality. It enhances narratives by translating concepts into strategic visual systems that operate between digital, print, spatial and audiovisual mediums, underlined by versatility and an expertise in emerging tools.

PP. 166-169

Pouya Ahmadi

be.net/pouyaahmadi

Pouya is a designer who explores typographic manifestations of hybrid and transnational identities. Featured in international exhibitions, publications, and design blogs, his work spans cultural and social fields, often involving collaborations with artists, curators, and designers.

PP. 580-583

Proyecto Ensamble

proyectoensamble.com

The first art toy-zine featuring contemporary artists and designers from Chile, Proyecto Ensamble is also a DIY platform for toy and 3-dimensional building blocks.

PP. 284-289

ps.2 arquitetura + design

ps2.com.br

Founded in 2003 by Fábio Prata and Flávia Nalon, ps.2 arquitetura + design is a São Paulo-based design studio working in both print and digital media for clients in the cultural field. Their award-winning work has also been published and exhibited worldwide.

PP. 516-519

reformer design studio

reformer.hk

reformer is a Hong Kong-based design studio founded by Wai Chan in 2012. It believes that design is not just for beautifying, but improving. Underlined by this philosophy and strong concepts, it works passionately to reform the world, focusing on typography and publication design.

PP. 392-395

Rice Creative

thisisrice.com

Rice Creative is a Ho Chi Minh-based branding and creative studio comprising a multicultural team with perspective and a precise vision. It adds value to bold brands through singular ideas, delivering powerful solutions with conviction and acclaimed craft.

PP. 350-353, 388-391

SANTAMBROGIOMILANO

santambrogiomilano.com

Founded in 2003, SANTAMBROGIOMILANO is a design company that works with glass – the magical element. Its first collection was born in 2004 with the first all-glass kitchen (designed by Ennio Arosio), pushing the boundaries of the design and production process over the years.

PP. 236-243

Shun-Zhi Yang
be.net/YANGSHUNZHI

Shun-Zhi Yang is a Taiwanese graphic designer who specialises in creating key visuals for exhibitions, books, music, and fine art. He believes that pain is the key to creating good design – and loves cats.

PP. 018-023

Sidi Vanetti
gysin-vanetti.com

Sidi is a graphic designer who runs his own visual communication studio and often collaborates with CCRZ on various projects.

PP. 372-373

Steven Wilson
stevenwilsonstudio.com

Born in London, Steven Wilson now lives and works in Brighton where he founded his studio in 2001. Working with Pedro Cardoso, Steven's output covers illustration, design, art direction, and animation. The duo continually experiment with techniques and processes to fuel their experimental work using analogue and digital tools.

PP. 294-297

stpmj

stpmj.com

stpmj is an idea-driven design practice based in New York and Seoul. Founded by Seung Teak Lee and Mi Jung Lim in 2009, they believe in exploring new perspectives built upon careful observations of materials, structures, and programmes based on social, cultural, political, environmental, and economic phenomena.

PP. 596-601

Studio Hausherr

ceeceecreative.com

Studio Hausherr was a graphic design agency in Berlin that specialised in corporate, editorial and web design for clients in art, fashion, and culture. As of 2016, it became part of Cec Cee Creative, a multidisciplinary agency focusing on consulting, design, content, and events.

PP. 500-501, 504-507

Studio Ongarato

studioongarato.com.au

Studio Ongarato is a multidisciplinary design studio based in Australia, Hong Kong, Dubai and the Americas with a portfolio of award-winning work, built on creative collaboration, strategic thinking and a holistic approach to design. Awarded Studio of the Year in 2017 by AGDA Design Awards, the studio is committed to innovation and bold thinking.

PP. 256-259

Syfon Studio

syfonstudio.com

Syfon Studio deals in visual interaction and creates cutting-edge visual concepts. The team believes that communication is a subtle and precise instrument that needs to be operated with knowledge and care. By analysing ongoing transformation processes and new media development, it considers design as an adventure.

PP. 110-111

Takeshi Kuroda (sandscape)

sandscape.biz

Based in Osaka, designer and artist Takeshi founded his studio to work on logotype, editorial, and graphic design. He has also worked on stage design with the ISHINHA theatrical company.

PP. 354-355

TENT

tent1000.com

Formed in 2011 by Masayuki Haruta and Ryosaku Aoki, TENT's work covers various fields including product, graphic, and packaging design, as well as retail, exhibition, and space design.

PP. 146-149

The Designers Republic™

thedesignersrepublic.com

The Designers Republic is a British graphic design studio based in Sheffield, founded in 1986 by Ian Anderson and Nick Phillips. They are best known for electronic music logos, album artwork, and anti-establishment aesthetics, embracing 'brash consumerism and the uniform style of corporate brands'.

PP. 158-159

The Gate Design Group

The Gate Design Group was an established design agency specialising in brand identities, web design and development, advertising, as well as editorial design and packaging with in-house photography facilities.

PP. 142-145

Thobias Studio

Founded by ESAG Penninghen graduates and art director-graphic designers Thibault Priou and Jonas Obadia, the studio was especially passionate about typography and editorial design.

PP. 298-301

TOKUJIN YOSHIOKA INC.

tokujin.com

Born in 1967, Tokujin Yoshioka worked under Shiro Kuramata and Issey Miyake before establishing his own studio, TOKUJIN YOSHIOKA INC. in 2000. Active in design, architecture, and contemporary art, his highly-acclaimed work is themed around nature and the Japanese idea of beauty.

PP. 223-235

Tomorrow Design Office

tomorrowdesign.hk

Tomorrow Design Office is an award-winning Hong Kong-based graphic design studio established in 2012. Specialising in visual communication, brand identities, packaging, marketing collaterals, and publications, it also launched PAPERIST, a self-initiated project to develop swatch books and other print-related products.

PP. 424-427

Triboro

triborodesign.com

Triboro is the award-winning Brooklyn-based design duo, David Heasty and Stefanie Weigler. Together, they create design solutions for clients in publishing, art, fashion, music, lifestyle, and cultural institutions. The studio excels in building inspiring brands from the ground up and shepherding established brands into new territories.

PP. 450-455

TwoPoints.Net

new.twopoints.net

TwoPoints.Net was founded in 2007 with the aim to do exceptional design work that is tailored to the client's needs, work that excites the client's customers, work that has not been done before, and work that does more than work.

Urška Jazbinšek, Anže Ermenc

Urška and Anže first met along the corridors of Križanke, where they were studying. Although they have different creative visions, the two have continued to join forces ever since.

Vrints-Kolsteren

vrints-kolsteren.com

Vrints-Kolsteren is an Antwerp-based design studio founded by Vincent Vrints and Naomi Kolsteren. Working locally and internationally, it offers creative direction, photography, and graphic design services by engaging in ongoing partnerships and creating a network of creative collaborators.

Yana Makarevich

be.net/yanamakarevich

Yana is a freelance designer and art director who has been working in branding since 2010, with interests that extend to strategy, positioning, advertising, and promotions.

PP. 196-205

Youhyeon Cho

be.net/u22hyeon7563

Youhyeon is a graphic designer in Seoul who works mainly with print, inspired by the meaning and materiality of things.

PP. 568-579

YOY

yoy-idea.jp

YOY is a Tokyo-based design studio headed by Naoki Ono, a spatial designer, and Yuki Yamamoto, a product designer. Founded in 2011, it creates new stories between spaces and objects.

PP. 560-561

Yu Hun Kim

yuhunkim.com

With a BA in Fine Art from Seoul as well as a BA in Furniture and Product Design from Kingston University, Yu Hun's approach to design is underlined by reinterpretations of her daily life and surroundings from an integrated viewpoint.

PP. 306-309

Zaha Hadid Architects

zaha-hadid.com

Founded by the late Zaha Hadid in 1979, the internationally renowned studio works on all scales and in all sectors to create transformative cultural, corporate, residential, and relevant spaces that work in synchronicity with their surroundings.

PP. 218-221

Zoo Studio

zoo.ad

Believing that good design lies in achieving the right equilibrium between aesthetics, functionality, innovation, technique, and simplicity, Zoo Studio is a multidisciplinary design studio in Barcelona that always strives to go further with each and every project.

PP. 276-279

Acknowledgements

We would like to specially thank all the designers
and studios who are featured in this book for their
significant contribution towards its compilation.
We would also like to express our deepest gratitude
to our producers for their invaluable advice and
assistance throughout this project, as well as the
many professionals in the creative industry who were
generous with their insights, feedback, and time.
To those whose input was not specifically credited or
mentioned here, we truly appreciate your support.

Future Editions

If you wish to participate in viction:ary's future projects
and publications, please send your portfolio to:
submit@victionary.com